HUMAN INTERESTS IN THE CURRICULUM

TEACHING AND LEARNING IN A TECHNOLOGICAL SOCIETY

Robert V. Bullough, Jr.
Stanley L. Goldstein
Ladd Holt

HUMAN INTERESTS IN THE CURRICULUM

Teaching and Learning in a Technological Society

HUMAN INTERESTS IN THE CURRICULUM,
Teaching and Learning in a Technological Society

Robert V. Bullough, Jr.
Stanley L. Goldstein
Ladd Holt
University of Utah

Teachers College, Columbia University
New York and London 1984

Published by Teachers College Press, 1234 Amsterdam Avenue, New York, N.Y. 10027

Library of Congress Cataloging in Publication Data

Bullough, Robert V.
  Human interests in the curriculum.

  Bibliography: p.
  Includes index.
1. Education—United States—Curricula. 2. School management and organization—United States. 3. Technocracy—Psychological aspects. I. Goldstein, Stanley L. II. Holt, Ladd.
III. Title.
LB1570.B88   1984   370.11′2   83-10063

ISBN 0-8077-2745-8

Manufactured in the United States of America

89 88 87 86   2 3 4 5 6

Contents

Preface

This book is an expression of the growth that has taken place in the authors as we have jointly struggled to understand some of our problems and frustrations as teachers and as teacher educators. The decision to produce it arose when we realized that our own continued growth necessitated doing more than reading and talking with one another; that it was time to make a statement that we hope will engender some interest on the part of those for whom we are most concerned: people contemplating entering teaching as a profession, those presently in programs of teacher education, young teachers, and people who are beginning to wonder about the quality of life lived in our nation's schools. We write to these individuals out of a commitment to the human intellect and spirit to confront the dehumanizing forces present in our society.

Over four years ago, the three of us came together to form a study group. We sought one another out for different reasons; perhaps we sensed a kind of like-mindedness though we were each serving in different divisions within the Graduate School of Education at the University of Utah. Our initial discussions revealed that we shared a general concern for the health of America and its institutions. But perhaps most fundamentally, we shared a concern for the health and vitality of the individual in an increasingly complex, mystifying, and hostile social environment. We also discovered that we shared a sense of professional isolation. As we have spoken to other teachers, we have found that our initial feelings of isolation were not, and are not, very much different from what many teachers at all levels of education feel.

We began by reading Marx's *The German Ideology*, and the *Manuscripts of 1844*. From there we went to volume 1 of *Capital*. Gradually our discussions increased in length and intensity as we saw how some of Marx's concepts elucidate present problems in the political economy. We began exploring the works of other authors that further explained and in some instances offered partial solutions to the problems Marx identified. Eventually we came to the work of Jurgen Habermas. We have found his work to be especially helpful in understanding the impact a kind of generalized positivistic attitude, what we will call *technocratic-mindedness*, has had on human life and institutions. The creation of this attitude is profoundly important for understanding schooling.

As we explored the meaning and implications of technocratic-mindedness, we became increasingly sensitive to its manifestations within our own lives and work. To further enhance our understanding and to further explore the connections we were beginning to see quite clearly between schooling and developments in advanced capitalism, we decided to go out into the field to talk with teachers. Chapter 2 is the result of this effort. Our initial hunches and fears were more than confirmed.

We offer this book as an extension of our own effort to understand. It has four primary purposes. First, we wish to introduce the reader to selected concepts that we have found useful in unraveling the complex manner in which the institutional structures of schools help to form and reinforce a particular set of attitudes and beliefs, a way of "seeing" the world, that is hostile to human freedom and development. Second, we want to make some of the taken-for-granted in education problematic in a way that will encourage the development of greater understanding. We are committed to the position that human intelligence can uncover and begin to remake those aspects of the social-economic-political life and personal life that are limiting to self and others. Third, our book is designed to serve as an example of what we are calling *critical* or *philosophical-mindedness*. And, finally, fourth, it will stand as a statement of hope without which there is silence, a deafening silence, that ensures defeat.

We wish to express our gratitude to Molly Campbell and staff for many hours spent typing various drafts of this manuscript. We must also acknowledge the many teachers, administrators, and district personnel who shared their time, materials, and much more with us. The openness with which we were received and the interest many of these people have shown in our work have been encouraging.

HUMAN INTERESTS IN THE CURRICULUM

Teaching and Learning in a Technological Society

Chapter 1

Minds, Schooling, and Critique

PREUNDERSTANDING

The concept denotated by the term *preunderstanding* is pivotal to our outlook. It may seem curious, perhaps even absurd, to speak of influential understandings that shape how and what we think yet are prior to our understanding. Actually the concept is not so obscure and can be made sense of in a rather straightforward, literal manner.

We always must use some kind of interpretive schema in order to perceive the world at all. By being born into a social context, we are also born into a constellation of shared meanings. These meanings, carried in various symbolic forms, verbal and nonverbal, orient us to the world in a manner deemed correct for our culture and language. Hence the initial categories with which we organize experience come from our immediate social-cultural contexts—family, religion, community, state, and so forth. From this way of conceiving preunderstanding, even so seemingly a natural principle of experiential organization as pain-pleasure takes on a social coloration. Early on, we learn the appropriate manly or womanly responses to these sensations and are expected to act accordingly. Long before we develop any reflective capacities, we are deeply embedded in a world of meaning that we must accept as our own.

Preunderstandings have three essential characteristics. First, they are *historical*. For the most part, preunderstandings are situated within a culture (local to universal) and change over time—albeit slowly. Emphatically, they are not to be seen as a priori givens embedded in the nature of things for all times and peoples. Second, they are necessary elements in all situations requiring understanding because they serve as a backdrop of meanings that *enable* understanding. Consider, in this regard, the fact that pictorial signs used by international airports to help people get around seem to be universally understandable. Third, preunderstandings *limit* and *distort* meaning because they significantly predetermine it by virtue of the world view and values inherent in a native language and a family and social context. Limitation and distortion come with the enabling characteristics of preunderstandings, for any particular view of things precludes or decries other possible views. These three formal components of preunderstandings occur simultaneously, of course, but not with equal emphasis.

The complex interrelationships among the historical, the enabling, and the limiting nature of preunderstandings are evident in many commonplace life occurrences. A good example is the crisis of faith often experienced by individuals when questions arise that are not adequately answered by the tenets of their religion. Since a religious orientation is generally the product of growing up in a family that held to these meanings, what comes to be questioned is not just the religion but what the parents are and the self they have helped to form. A crisis of faith results when religious meanings do not harmonize with new ideas. In order to produce more harmony, the individual in crisis may confront his own history and choose to reconstruct it—he may come to see it in a new and different light. For some the result of this process may lead to rejection; for others faith is reasserted though its justification may be changed. In this process it is possible to uncover the content and form of our preunderstandings and to subject them to scrutiny. The possibility arises through our efforts to resolve contradictions that we find when what we assumed to be the case proves inadequate in accounting for events.

Replacing preunderstandings with new understandings usually involves considerable mental effort and emotional tension as certainties become ambiguous and then discredited. The key point is that the one— preunderstandings — is thrust on us whereas the other — gaining new understanding—involves degrees of deliberate choice. Preunderstandings are unconscious, pervasive influences that can be understood for what they are only as they are brought to consciousness and articulated. Michael Polanyi describes this movement of human intelligence as making "tacit" knowledge "explicit."[1] Both are necessary, but only explicit knowledge lends itself to revision.

Different historical-cultural settings produce different preunder-

standings with which people are born, live, and die. However, this fact
and the fact that preunderstandings can be annulled do not weaken the
power of their hold on us. Consider, for example, our conceptions of time.
Most of us in industrialized cultures grow up thinking of time in linear
terms. We become clock watchers and organize our activities around the
movements of the clock. Few of us ever pause to wonder what this kind of
organization does to the quality of our lives. Instead we accept it as a given
and either fight with or race against the clock, complaining all the while
about how little time we have and how much we need to get done. We
accept as natural—even though potentially detrimental to our good health
— an organization of time that is culturally embedded and imposed.
Cultures that do not share our preunderstandings organize time in different
ways. Some organize it around the changing seasons, some around the
phases of the moon, still others around the cycles of life. They too take
their preunderstandings as natural and proper.

That our preunderstandings are historical helps to elucidate the
nature and source of some of the conflicts we encounter in class-based and
in pluralistic societies. In pluralistic societies conflicts abound when the
shared views that have maintained group aspirations by defining individual ambitions break down. This is often seen in the problems associated
with religious, ethnic, and racial intermarriage. Similarly socioeconomic
classes provide their preunderstandings too. (As F. Scott Fitzgerald
quipped, "The rich are just like everyone else, only different!") For
instance, consider what happens when two strangers from disparate backgrounds and training meet on a bus. Immediately they recognize their
differences and probably attempt to avoid one another. If they must talk,
they are often awkward and uncomfortable, and their communication is
hindered by their slightly different vocabularies or word meanings. In
short their taken-for-granted values drive a wedge between them.

Nevertheless, in spite of such class-connected limitations, these
individuals most likely share general cultural preunderstandings that
ultimately enable them to interact if they must. They probably have
roughly similar economic, political, and social values and concerns. They
worry about unemployment and nuclear arms, watch the same programs on
television, likely shop at the same kind of stores, have common recrea-
tional and sports interests, and work in similarly organized establish-
ments. They have, in a sense, been brought together by the nature of life
within Western society. By virtue of this circumstance, we participate in
what Don Ihde calls a *technosphere*, which unites us in a common history at

a most fundamental level.[2] Thus while there will be important differences in our tacit understandings because of differences in backgrounds and social positions, we are yet more tightly bound together by a set of preunderstandings as a consequence of growing up in a technologically dominated, growth-oriented, advanced industrial society.

The limiting and enabling functions of preunderstandings become more recognizable in situations where tacit understandings resulting from personal histories prove incongruent with the culturally dominant meanings embedded in institutions and practices. For instance, what happens to our two bus riders if the individual representing the lower-status position refuses to defer and is not heedful of traditional status symbols?

Tensions resulting from conflicts between personal and larger cultural values abound in schools. When a young person enters a classroom, she enters a value-laden environment that may or may not square with her own values. The teacher, a central component in the environment, and the structure of the institution itself—how it is organized, what is excluded and included, role expectations, and the like — press a message of what is desirable, right, and true. This message is consistent with the work requirements of the larger society that the schools serve. When students can share this world of meanings, many of which are implicit and operate as preunderstandings, they will be more or less at home. They intuitively understand what teachers and administrators are trying to do to and for them and generally accept the reasons given for these actions. They see the established power relationships as legitimate. In this situation there is pervasive, unarticulated, and deep-lying agreement on the rules of interaction. These rules are assumed, and interaction is comparatively easy. Communication is *enabled* by the continuity of understandings and preunderstandings. But this kind of communication is not always possible, for teachers also encounter students who do not possess the attitudes deemed essential for school success. They get labeled as unmotivated or troubled, and the source of the problem is usually located within the student. The tacit and explicit institutional values that operate through teachers and administrators *limit* the ways in which such problems may be identified and solved. In fact some actions are identified as problems that in other contexts would be ignored or praised. We assume, for example, that the student who does not do well in school is in error when the difficulty may stem from a discontinuity between her values and beliefs and the values embedded in the institution of schooling. What is perhaps most important here is that neither the student nor the teacher understands what is happening; each assumes how she sees things is correct. A difference, however, arises because the teacher has the weight of the educational establishment behind her view.

Students identified as troubled or unmotivated may respond to the efforts of teachers and administrators to get them into line—to motivate them—in a variety of ways. One of the most potent is to reject various aspects of life within schools. Such students generally continue to attend but they do so with reluctance and to the displeasure of teachers. However, while these students stand as a challenge to the values of the school, they ultimately find themselves further enmeshed in them. At first glance the idea that rejection should result in acceptance appears contradictory. It is not.[3] For example, students who act out their distaste for the conformity required for success in school find themselves counseled into special programs that prepare them to work in vocations that are themselves highly controlled and of relatively low status. The plea for relevant education is answered with programs that serve to strengthen the rejected values. The critical capacity of teachers and students alike is neutralized, and institutional values are reinforced. Those who choose to leave school soon discover that what they have rejected now must be accepted in order that they may feed and clothe themselves. Rather ironically then, while many students reject school, a few with considerable insight into the implicit value structure of schooling, they ultimately find themselves co-opted into relations they had expected to avoid. In rejecting school they also reject the possibility it offers to be educated. Hence the power and prevalence of preunderstandings remain secure because those who might have provided a challenge are rendered ineffective by it.

It is our position that the most fundamental preunderstanding in modern industrialized countries is the technocratic ideology. Its pervasiveness significantly constrains the enabling or communicative function of preunderstandings along particular paths. When communication is so severely restricted at this deep level, both cultural and individual crises may follow as our isolation from one another becomes more stringently marked and more difficult to break through. For some the resulting sense of loss calls for strengthening dominant values and approved meanings. For others it is the impetus to question, to try to create new meanings and values. In our view the crisis is here; it exists now in contemporary culture. At present schooling, intentionally and unintentionally, plays an important role in reproducing technocratic values. Nevertheless, public education still remains one of the hopeful means for fostering a human world. In order to help realize this ideal, we must create visions of public education that are not so bounded but are open to a myriad of possibilities.

TECHNOCRATIC-MINDEDNESS

In discussing human needs, Jurgen Habermas offers a useful categorization. He suggests that we can speak about humans in terms of possessing three broad interests: work, communication, and emancipation.[4] By our work interest, Habermas means those activities involved in satisfying physical needs: food, shelter, and so on. These activities are directed toward the control and manipulation of the natural environment. Our communication interest is concerned with the desire to understand and be understood. Our emancipation interest centers on our drive to transcend, to grow and develop.

In serving our work interest, science and technology and the rationality they embody have proven themselves powerful tools. However, this has been a mixed blessing. The nature of this ambivalence has more to it than the rather obvious but important problems of pollution and nuclear proliferation. What has happened is that we have adopted the form of rationality associated with realizing our work interest, what Habermas calls *instrumental rationality*, as the appropriate form of rationality for satisfying all our interests. But instrumental rationality has become more than a tool for solving problems; it is a mindedness lodged in a set of vital preunderstandings.

To set off instrumental rationality as a tool from instrumental rationality as a set of preunderstandings, we use the term *technocratic-mindedness*. This distinction is necessary because in some areas of human experience, instrumental rationality is apt and important. Difficulties arise, however, when a single mode of interaction with the world, a single form of rationality, dominates to the exclusion of other modes. In this case things are askew because technical action replaces reflection and communicative interaction when these are most needed.

But what does it mean to be technocratically minded? Technocratic-mindedness is indicated by an uncritical acceptance of the view that only the methods of a narrow conception of science produce genuine knowlege. Furthermore, it is assumed that the only appropriate way to solve our social-political-ethical problems is by applying the methods of science to these problems. Hence there is, on the part of the technocratically minded, an exclusive concern with measurement, prediction, control, efficiency, and governance by experts in addressing all human problems. From this standpoint the proper political involvement of the public is choosing between options proposed by experts. Once the public has made its choice, it then falls to these same experts to carry out the preferred option. Value issues—those in the realms of the social, the political, the ethical, and the educational — get reduced to technical questions. The concern is not what *should* be done but rather how it *can* be done. Those issues that do not respond to technical treatment are relegated to the sphere of mere opinion. When a proposed solution fails, the problem is located not in the goals but only in the means selected to achieve them. This results in calls for greater expertise and less involvement of individuals lacking the desired skills.

An excellent example of how technocratic-mindedness functions in schools is provided by the use and importance of standardized testing. Objective testing is predicated on the assumption that "whatever exists at all, exists in some amount" and "can be measured."[5] Further, for schooling purposes, the quantity of something is its most important aspect. Obviously not everything that a person experiences in school is or can be subjected to testing. A child is not tested on whether or not she places her tray in the proper location upon leaving the lunchroom. Nor is a student tested on the quality of the conversations he has in the hallway with his friends. The first example is trivial while the latter is perhaps fundamentally important for student growth and development. The assumption is, however, that it is possible to test those things that are central to the mission of the school, especially in the areas of knowledge and skill. Already the view of what happens in school, what is considered educative, has been significantly narrowed to those things that are related to the formal subject matter of the curriculum. This range of testable material is still further reduced by the simple recognition that no usable test can measure all that can be known by a person in a subject area; there are managerial and time considerations that must be attended to. Testmakers therefore select a small sample of content to measure and, through statistical means, relate the sample to the total amount known. Textbooks, or more accurately, published programs, are taken as the embodiment of knowledge in an area and systematically sampled to identify bits of content for testing. Possible items are carefully written and studied and tried out in test situations with students. Finally, those test items that have the best technical qualities appear in the final form of a standardized test.

This process is carefully employed by measurement experts so that the final items are a representative sample of the information in the major published programs. The technical sophistication tends to disguise the actual procedures of test production, thereby according the tests an apparently all-encompassing power to measure a person's knowledge with precision. Such tests communicate a taken-for-granted view of both the nature of knowledge and learning. Knowledge is a series of known statements about some part of reality, and learning is determined by the ability to recognize these statements when presented with the proper stimulus—in this case a multiple choice question. The rather straightforward outlook is that the truth is known and is found in textbooks. Following this line of reasoning, education, to a considerable extent, is learning to read and remember.

Because the standardized test is seen as something that measures knowledge, the success of teaching and learning is determined by how well students perform on the test. To guarantee success the teacher needs to teach for the test, to make certain that the sample of content on the test is taught as the most significant part of the curriculum. Successful students must also focus upon learning the items that are to be tested. Under such a system, tests become mythologized. They are seen as containing powers that in actuality they do not possess, and learning can become trivialized because it is focused upon a narrow band of information that at best is a small sample of what is worth knowing. The subtle, complex, personally selective, often confusing, and sometimes sublime task of coming to know is converted into a linear system of selecting the correct responses to a series of multiple choice questions. Knowledge becomes a specific number telling you how much you know and how your amount of knowledge is comparable to that possessed by others. When such instruments are built and used, knowing becomes sterile and the knower becomes an object that can be defined by a number. For both teachers and students, education is reduced to training and teaching is management of persons and things. Hence our communication and emancipation interests become limited to and defined by our work interest and the instrumental rationality associated with it.

By the emphasis placed on the objectivity of a technical procedure to certify that someone has learned, standardized tests become a means of social control. They document that a person has learned the socially necessary. Moreover, that selection of knowledge also determines to a considerable extent the relationship that students will have with the information presented—uncritical acceptance and incorporation. But this need not be the case.

CRITICAL-MINDEDNESS

Whereas technocratic-mindedness indicates an unconscious and therefore uncritical apprehension of what is considered natural or the way things really are and the way they must be, an opposite state is also possible. We can be *critically* or *philosophically minded*. That is, we can rationally scrutinize what is taken as being natural for individuals and for social life. In the Western tradition—at least as far back as Plato—reason is held to be an inherent human capacity that springs to life only when one experiences doubt or uncertainty, when there is a need to clear up perplexity, to make sense of things for oneself. Being critically minded means nothing more than exercising our innate potential to reason, to pause and think about things. Critical-mindedness is best characterized as a questioning attitude, a call for the reasons why of a situation. This attitude was given its classic form in Socrates' famous claim that "to let no day pass without discussing goodness and all the other subjects . . . is really the very best thing a man can do, and that life without this sort of examination is not worth living."[6] Socrates emphasizes that the philosophic or critical attitude requires discussion of issues, especially those involving our value judgments. Discussion means communication. It signals a process of mutual respect, of mutuality of purpose, of openness toward the discovery of what had been hidden from view. It requires that we attempt to see things differently. Discussion, dialogue, and communication—that is, the exercise of our rational or critical capacities—is action toward liberation.

By way of illustration, let us consider once again the powerful influence of standardized testing in the world of the professional educator. In this professional world of ours, we by and large take test results as gospel. We assume they show us reality, the way things actually are. We faithfully accept, for example, that a certain numeral or position on a graph *is* Jane's native intelligence or what she really understands about mathematics or geography or biology even when those results do not accord with our experience of her abilities and understanding. We know that the tests give us facts; they need not and ought not to be questioned. The strain we sense between cognition and experience is suppressed. We explain away any discrepancy between our feelings and estimations about Jane and the standardized test results as stemming from our own shortcomings; we are not objective enough to be scientific and thus unable to see things as they really are. Besides, to raise questions about this discrepancy is time-consuming, and inevitably we will be proven incorrect.

In this typical situation, such flickering doubt as we may have about the reality of Jane fades under the authority of testing. Without comment we acquiesce to the expert's picture of Jane by neglecting to discuss the differences that exist between our understanding of her and the view presented to us. Initially, perhaps, we would want to mull the differences over, then discuss them with others who know her. The important point is that unless something like this goes on, the issue does not get examined; it is lost, and the truth of things—Jane's abilities—has been defined for us and for Jane by an impersonal source far removed from both of us.

This situation is a common one in the work of teachers wherein critical-mindedness or its absence bears heavily on the conduct of classroom practice. Let us now consider in more depth what is involved in being critically or philosophically minded. Again, we must stress that our concern is with life in schools as it is lived.

There is nothing mysterious about the reflective or critical process. It is something we all engage in from time to time in our daily lives when habits fail to serve our needs. Consider, by way of simple illustration, how we use a flashlight or a cigarette lighter. Normally we push the button for light or spin the wheel for a flame and do not give the device any or much conscious attention. The actions we use to get these things to work are habitual actions. However, should the flashlight or lighter fail to perform its function, we are forced by circumstances to pay attention to it. We may respond unthinkingly to this problem by simply and habitually replacing the batteries. But if this more or less automatic response fails, we must become conscious of the device and start to evaluate other possible sources of failure. It is at this point we begin to think about or reflect on how the device normally works and how it might be inhibited from working. The effort to determine the causes of the device's malfunctioning is an example —mundane and somewhat technical in character, to be sure—of our capacity to be reflective, thoughtful, or even, in a broad sense, philosophical. It is a capacity called forth by the press of events when reality and a desired state of affairs are at odds.

While we all have this potential, it is clear that there is wide variation in situations that will prompt us to engage in the critical process as well as wide variation in the skill of critical thinking. There is, for example, clearly a strong qualitative dimension to being critically minded. Some do it better than others, and doing it better involves more knowledge about the issue and more familiarity with the practice. Doing and knowing are mutually and simultaneously enhancing in this activity. To resort to the example of the flashlight once again, if I do not know anything about electricity or even just about flashlights, I will not have much to mull over when its malfunctioning has become a problem for me. In ignorance my solution to the difficulty might be to throw the thing away in a rage, or throw up my hands and accept the inconvenience as the "way things are." With knowledge the potential for overcoming my difficulty is enhanced. But let us be cautious here. For though we are arguing that more knowledge is necessary, we recognize that knowledge by itself is insufficient to guarantee critical-mindedness or high quality critical thinking.

That there is a wide variety in what individuals consider problematic is a commonplace. Clearly vast differences in training, experience, and intellectual capacity exist among humans. We would not normally expect a young person who recently graduated from a vocationally oriented, inner city high school to demonstrate a critical capacity equal to that of a highly educated graduate of a distinguished college humanities program—though it is certainly possible. But because we take it for granted that we are all different, have different experiences, and therefore different problems, we tend to emphasize our dissimilarities at the expense of our more fundamental commonalities. Besides the more obvious problems we share due to our biology, there are those we share (as we discussed earlier) because we live in a technocratically dominated culture. Unfortunately, our concern over differences, which are often superficial, serves to mask the common nature of the barriers we experience in understanding one another. The cultural emphasis on individual differences helps keep us strangers; it helps make us believe that individual inadequacies are the source of our problems in understanding and controlling our world. Yet if emancipation is to flourish, we must break down this barrier through recognizing our mutual identity in the need to overcome social, political, economic, and professional domination.

In this attitude of recognizing our mutual need, we also see that there are many levels of interpretation among us and therefore many possible entry points into uncovering or demystifying that which limits our comprehension and inhibits our control. The essential factor in a demystifying process is movement toward expanded understanding and control that is guided by a notion of enhanced human freedom and dignity. The process of uncovering what frustrates our efforts to promote freedom and dignity begins, we have been arguing, in raising questions. But what instigates the questioning of that which *usually passes unnoticed?* Some things work well at one level, say technically, but nonetheless are disquieting at another, perhaps in an emotional sense.

A rather common situation encountered by student teachers as they begin their in-school work illustrates the point. Teacher-training programs typically instruct trainees in how to write behavioral or performance objectives. This instruction is presented for a variety of public reasons: It is assumed that clear objectives aid in planning coherent lessons, that objectives stated in terms of student performance lend themselves to the making of precise judgments about student progress, and that in general, objectives can and should be determined in advance of instruction by teachers or curriculum specialists. All in all, it is believed that objectives stated in behavioral or performance terms—for example, "The student will correctly identify, at the 80-percent level, the following verb tenses: _____"—are the most useful. In short they are supposed to facilitate teaching and learning.

Before doing her student teaching, a trainee, through practice, develops a modicum of skill in writing such objectives and includes them in the units she is required to write for her methods courses. Eventually she enters a school as a student teacher, or intern carrying a unit or two she has previously designed. It is not long, however, before she begins to realize that even her best objectives do not always represent what the students are supposed to learn and that some students achieve an objective but still lack understanding. A discontinuity is felt. Skill in writing objectives has proven to be somewhat inadequate to the situation. The objectives, much like the flashlight, do not work as they are supposed to, or work only inter-mittently. However, discontinuity may also arise where performance objectives seem to work but the format itself does not allow inclusion of highly prized content and experiences. Perhaps the student teacher recognizes that her objectives focus upon what proves to be the more trivial aspects of her interaction with pupils and that she really cannot use them and still get at what strikes her as educationally significant. At this point she faces a dilemma; how she responds to it will either enable or limit her further development.

On the one hand, she might locate the problem in her own inadequacies or her students' lack of motivation. She could then decide to work even harder to write better objectives and perhaps manipulate the situation so that it fits the skill, thereby eliminating the problem. A response of this kind reinforces the preunderstanding. On the other hand, she might opt to continue planning carefully but begin to write objectives that express her values and include phrases like "appreciating a story" or "enjoying music." She would trust that she would be able to tell when students were realizing her aims. Where appropriate, she would continue to use performance objectives, but she would become increasingly intelligent about their limitations. When objectives got in the way of her conception of what is worth learning, she would disregard the format. A response of this kind suggests that the individual's critical capacity has come into play.

Teaching abounds in such situations where discontinuity, contradiction, and paradox arise. Whether or not a discrepancy will be noted and whether or not it will become a problem largely depend upon our perceiving that our interests are in some way jeopardized by the discrepancy. (*Interest* should be understood in the broadest sense to include ideals, aims, values, and the like.) The behavioral objective example illustrates our point. For student teachers who clearly recognize the limitations and strengths of the behavioral objective approach to planning, the dominating interest seems to be a desire to maintain a maximum degree of flexibility and openness in the teaching-learning situation. They refuse to let their interaction with students be bounded by their objectives; other important and sometimes unpredicted learning opportunities emerge that make in-school life more interesting for them and the students. For student teachers who choose to manipulate the situation to fit their developed skill, we can fairly say that the primary interest displayed is maintaining predictability and control. This response may be a reflection of a commitment to a particular view of the desirable teacher-student relation or an expression of fear in the event things might somehow get out of control, resulting in a poor supervisor evaluation.

Thus whether an incongruity is grasped as a problem and held as problem-relevant to our professional interests will depend upon our values and standards of judgment. The extent to which any situation draws our attention seems inherently tied to our normative outlook; that is, to how we think schools should operate or what life in the classroom ought to be, to our professional standards and ideals and values in general, to our vision of the best way for people and institutions to interact.

But if we are dominated by a technocratic-mindedness that operates at the level of preunderstanding, how is such discontinuity and conflict even possible? Let us recall that there is a range of human interests, which we earlier classified as our communication and emancipation interests, that transcends the boundaries of our technical interest. These categories of interest cannot be satisfied or expressed by the rationality embodied in technocratic-mindedness. Our makeup is such that the principal characteristics of human reason—a technical interest, a communicative interest, and an emancipatory interest—can be at odds with one another. We may be pulled toward different values, goals, or procedures by our reason. There is therefore inner conflict, doubt, discontinuity, and questions about which way to go. Moreover, the goals built into technocratic-mindedness for human interaction and institutional functioning, which many of us easily accept—goals such as efficiency, predictability, and controllability—are seldom realizable to the desired level or degree. We are not, after all, machines, and attempts to structure human activity in terms that are appropriate for inanimate objects are bound to create discrepancies between expectation and reality. Hence discontinuity occurs because of the tensions that stem from the need to exercise our interest in surviving, communicating, and being free of domination and because of actual failures in realizing the values associated with technocratic-mindedness.

Frequently we describe the discontinuities and problems that arise from ignorance about the exercise of our communicative-interactive interest as a metaphorical blindness. We speak of being unable to "see" the obstructions to understanding or making sense of our experience. Conversely, when we gain understanding, we speak of "having insight," "getting clear about things," "shedding blinders," "seeing it," and similar phrases. Disclosing that which blocks our understanding is the interest of reason at work trying to overcome various dominations. It is one of the human needs that goads reason into action, that starts up the questioning process so crucial to examining experience.

We make sense of our experience by imposing order on it. But "Whose order?" is the vital question. It makes all the difference whether that order is the one embedded in the preunderstanding—therefore the accepted or dominant view—or if it is one wrested from reflection upon the accepted view and what our needs and values require. The preunderstanding gives us ready-made categories for achieving coherence. In teaching it allows us to accept at face value categories like the "hyperactive child," which carries with it a structure of order that includes faith in the expert to tell us the way things are and faith in the truth of dealing with children in terms of objective abstractions. The alternative to dealing with children in such a way is to have thought about and be actively thinking about how children learn and how they can and do interact with others and with ideas, and how this affects one's own conception of the aims of education. This is precisely becoming critically minded or philosophically minded about education because it is thinking about the norms that prescribe how we should value our experience. It means thinking about what should concern us and with what emphasis. For the teacher critical thinking about education means struggling with a probably vague conception of educational aims and professional standards. Teachers who are consciously struggling with their professional standards and educational aims can exercise skepticism about the so-called normal or acceptable professional outlook (e.g., the "hyperactive child") whenever it does not coincide with the standards and aims they are trying to forge. Critically minded teachers begin to understand that the dominant outlook on what is proper order in education expresses the value system of the preunderstanding but is not to be accorded superior status because of it. Rather they become aware that this outlook serves class interests for domination because they start to see that the preunderstanding is necessarily the foundation of the status quo.

However, this level of understanding is not gained easily. Our critically minded teachers did not achieve their perspective without effort. For although we have claimed that being philosophic is an inherent human possibility that we need to exercise, we have also argued that social, political, and economic interests whose legitimacy stems from the preunderstanding constrain the cultivation of the philosophic potential. Because the preunderstanding provides us with a ready-made orientation to what is real, natural, and acceptable, it sets certain limitations to the way problems and the possibility of their resolution can be seen. In effect it tells us what our problems can be and what are acceptable solutions to them. But the given view is itself problematic because our perceptual apparatus seems incapable of grasping its limitations. It is difficult to get "new eyes," so to speak, that will enable us to see things from a perspective that challenges or even contradicts the one we were born into. It means taking the world view that was natural, correct, and right for us and declaring it now unnatural and incorrect, at least in part.

A recent teaching experience of one of the authors illustrates the difficulty of seeing anew as well as indicating how that seeing, and hence philosophic-mindedness, may be encouraged. In one of our classes, a group of elementary school teachers was writing about the influences of business ideology on the aims and practices of public education today. They could all readily give some current examples of this influence. This part of the writing was easy for them. But they wanted to say more; they wanted to say something critical about the situation and could not. Lodged within their descriptions of business influence was an implicit but unarticulatable criticism of this state of affairs. Virtually every essay implied that something was wrong with an educational situation in which educators' needs and standards were clearly subordinate to a set of demands having nothing to do with educational values. For two reasons these teachers could only hint at the sense of discrepancy they felt. On the one hand, they lacked the concepts necessary for framing a criticism of this fact of educational life. On the other hand, expression was inhibited by the lack of a conscious grasp of their own educational values. Most importantly, they had not tried to make explicit their implicit beliefs about the aims and means of education. When they confronted a situation that was problematic —as when they sensed the inappropriateness of the commercial influence on education — they lacked the means for saying what was wrong, why there was a problem. But if they had grasped their educational values more consciously, they would have been able to point out the difference between the priorities of educators and businessmen. And if, in addition, they had held a critical perspective on their work, they could have deepened their analysis, disclosing the properties of capitalism that require such influence from business enterprise.

Had we ended our considerations of the topic with the writing assignment, very little would have been done to foster critical-mindedness. In general the felt discrepancies would have remained hidden from view, still only vaguely sensed. Some, perhaps, would have wrestled with the disturbance they experienced, but most would have let it all slip out of consciousness as they turned their attention to the myriad demands teachers face. But our presence in a class together was a medium for making the vaguely sensed and unsayable both more clearly understood and expressible. Our discussion brought the character of the discrepancies into the light. Words and ideas that had been elusive started coming as we engaged in dialogue and helped one another clarify and define the disturbing ambiguities. The process was one of respectful, serious questioning directed toward clearer understanding. In the Socratic tradition, dialogue was the midwife of critical comprehension.

There is a twofold importance to this dialogic process. Participation in communicative interaction is the way to develop philosophic-mindedness. Asking questions to get clearer about issues, topics, doubts, and disturbances is a genuine philosophic activity, and practicing it is being critically minded. Thus the process itself has a developmental payoff in respect to critical-mindedness; it helps nourish it. In addition the insight gained as a result of this interactive process also has its developmental effects. For understanding has been enhanced by what one has learned, by what one is now able to express. As a consequence of the process, more knowledge is available to bring to bear on problems. Resources for seeing into felt discrepancies and for stating their problematic aspects have been augmented. And in fact this seemed to be the case with our class of teachers. Subsequent discussions of topics involving educational values started out from a more sophisticated point, and they proceeded in a more question-raising, dialogic manner than before. This certainly seemed to be a promising beginning to the crucial educational task of encouraging the growth of critical-mindedness.

Let us say a final word about some of the characteristics of a teacher's work environment that can encourage philosophic-mindedness. It is undoubtedly true that teachers' days are increasingly crowded with clerking tasks, leaving them little time to address their own sense of what should be learned next. It is also true that technocratic-mindedness is a formidable impediment to recognizing the large number of opportunities for thinking critically that are ever present in teaching. Nevertheless certain objective conditions about teaching and teachers lend hope to our vision of developing critical-mindedness in the profession. Teachers, after all, are educated people. Practicing teachers have gone to a university or college, read books, listened to and tried to understand ideas different from their own, and had to express their own points of view on a variety of topics. They have had to use their minds on the way to becoming teachers, and they have used them in the daily communicative interactions that teaching still calls for now and again. Even though their work days may be prescribed to a great extent, certain decisions yet must be made by individual teachers. When time constraints make it necessary to eliminate some part of a curriculum, teachers have to make a choice. This requires exercising a measure of reflection in order to justify that decision: Why this story? Why this activity? Why these problems and not others? In the same way, teachers must make choices about appropriate forms of discipline to use with individuals and the class. They have to decide the best way to motivate one student and the fair grade for another. And the subtler dynamics of the warmth or distance that should color individual class-teacher relationships are concerns that must be thought about from time to time. Of course, any or all teaching decisions may be made with only a modicum of

conscious attention. Reasons for a decision may be poor—choosing to re-
tain or drop a facet of curriculum solely on time requirements, say, disre-
garding any educational values. But then, reducing this possibility is precisely the point of trying to develop critical-mindedness among teachers.
As we have been arguing throughout this discussion, the best safeguard
against the dull, repetitive training that passes for public education and
that reduces a teacher's work to the mechanical management of prepack-
aged routines is the enhancement of the critical, reflective potential that
resides in all of us and pervades the very nature of the educative process.

CONCLUSION

We have argued that there is no such thing as individual emancipation separate from the emancipation of others. Freedom and emancipation
are at heart social concepts that inform our thinking and doing at every
level of life—in our families, with our colleagues, friends, students, and
strangers, and in the political domain. Our interest in a humane life necessarily rests with others. At present a destructive emphasis on individualism has emerged. It plays on human greed, promising power and the
furthering of selfish interests. It is a false individualism, arising from
alienation, which demands unquestioning acceptance of the programs and
values of technocrats. So while the rhetoric that rallies assent is about
human freedom, the action and the effect are toward greater domination, however pleasantly and seductively presented. A more genuine concern for the individual recognizes the shared nature of most of our problems and the necessity of entering into mutually enhancing growth-
producing relations with others, what we call *dialogic relations*. Such relations are necessary conditions for the full development of critical-mindedness; they enable critical thought to move outward into the realm of political action, an important facet of living ethically. This dialogue and ethical
action is directed at helping us see the limitations on our emancipatory
interest. With better understanding comes the possibility of bringing our
institutions into closer accord with our communicative and emancipatory
interests. We begin by first talking about those vaguely sensed discontinuities that arise so frequently in our work, attempting to tease out their
origin and meaning in discussion with others. Where we end is uncertain.

We have discussed how preunderstandings operate both to constitute
and to limit our knowledge. We have argued that the dominant set of pre-

understandings in Western culture predisposes us to a way of seeing and interacting with the world that we have called technocratic-mindedness. We have claimed that this mindedness is not the natural and inevitable consequence of the structure of things but is rather a particular product of historical development, hence open to modification. Further, we have suggested that one effect of this mindedness has been the emergence of a constricted view of the meaning of education and of the possible approaches to creating educative environments. Specifically, our traditional liberal arts emphasis on esthetic, moral, and cognitive education has been replaced by a concern for training modeled on a factory-production view of control and efficiency. In short, with our current emphasis on training, we have reached the educational limits of the structures we have created to carry our educational ideals to fruition. Our mindedness now limits our ability to think and act in fresh ways and to grow cognitively, esthetically, and morally. Other visions of possibility are necessary. Finally, we have located the source of fresh visions in the consciousness that contradicts the technocratic orientation, in what we have been calling critical- or philosophic-mindedness.

In the chapters that follow, we will raise questions about the taken-for-granted in five school programs that are national in scope or intent. In raising these questions, our purpose is not only to uncover some of the workings of technocratic-mindedness but also to demonstrate the possibilities for revitalizing our educational vision that can flow from a critical perspective. Often we react to the word *critical* by dismissing it as merely a cynic's efforts to make his destructive outlook seem intellectual and reasonable. Certainly to be critical is to be destructive. But criticism destroys in a positive sense too, for it uncovers the meanings that have limited our understanding and unnecessarily restricted our actions. In this positive sense, criticism of the taken-for-granted signals the awakening of new understandings and unaccustomed actions that will better serve our vital interests.

Chapter 2

The Rational Curriculum: Teachers and Alienation

The preferred form or pattern of curriculum development in the United States includes preestablished, carefully sequenced and measurable objectives and heavy reliance upon standardized testing for proof of learning. Analysis of GEMS (Goal-Based Educational Management System), an example of the pattern, and the reactions of the teachers working in the program illuminates the character and influence of technocratic-mindedness in education.

THE FORMAL CURRICULUM

Rapid and uneven population growth, a comparatively young and inexperienced faculty, tight budgets, and a concern for mastery of the so-called basics provided reasons for the Jordan School District to develop GEMS, a new, more uniform and rational curriculum. For the public perhaps the most compelling reason was that students' achievement test scores were not sufficiently high. The argument for change seems to have gone something like this: (1) students are not learning the basic skills well enough (particularly reading and mathematics); (2) the proof of the claim is declining test scores; (3) test scores indicate the areas that need improvement; (4) this is best achieved by carefully systematizing content and activities; and (5) to ensure content mastery, student progress has to be constantly evaluated. This argument is based upon several assumptions about the purpose of schools, human learning, knowledge, and teaching. The assumptions are evident in the formal curriculum plan developed by the district and in the informal curriculum, what teachers and students actually do.

The formal curriculum is illustrated in model 1. The instructional goals are the most important part of the model. They are stated behaviorally in terms that reflect program (rather than learner) requisites and are easy to evaluate. The behavioral objectives represent that portion of content and skills deemed essential for students to master in a given period. Hence each grade has an assigned number of objectives to be mastered before students can advance to the next grade. The student's work is divided into units—clusters of objectives—that are keyed to tests. Pretests indicate how much a student knows prior to beginning a unit. If he scores 80 percent or above on the pretest, it is assumed that he has "mastered" that content, and he proceeds to the next unit in the sequence. A score of less than 80 percent requires additional study and retaking the test.

Pretests are used to group students. In theory it is conceivable that no two would be at exactly the same point in their progress toward mastery though in practice ability grouping and group teaching are necessary. The primary concern of instruction is to get a proper fit between learning materials, activities — coded in advance to a particular level of student

MODEL 1.   *GEMS Instructional Model*

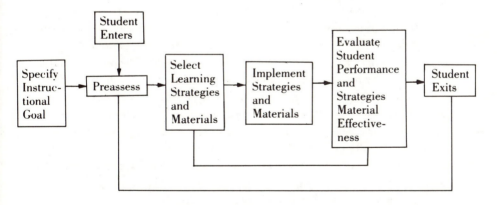

Source: Reprinted by permission of Jordan School District, Sandy, Utah.

learning—and the students' needs, that is, what must be known to pass the test. Those who achieve mastery after studying the unit move on while those who fail are taught the content again, presumably in a different way. Thus a student works from day to day and year to year through various contents until all the essential skills, facts, and concepts have been learned.

This approach to curriculum rests upon seldom questioned preunderstandings manifested in the assumptions of behavioral psychology and industrial management that justify a particular conception of educational efficiency. For example, while the instructional model does not include a broad statement of goals, one exists. Interestingly, it is not included because supposedly broad educational goals are not important to teachers or students who are properly concerned only with the specific objectives toward which they must work.

The relationship between stating goals and writing behavioral objectives is crucial to an understanding of how curriculum development under this approach is a technical process. Goals are stated in broad terms and reflect a general consensus about what should be accomplished in school. The emphasis on consensus is important because conflict might be destabilizing and system threatening. School goals will therefore include something for everyone. For example, the district's curriculum goals included the "development of competency in basic skills" and "the development of pride in work and a feeling of self-worth."[1] Probably all of the patrons would agree that schools should strive to reach these goals. But what do they mean?

Goals are statements of value viewed by technocrats as nothing more than matters of opinion because there is no scientific procedure for determining their validity. Any value or goal is therefore only a matter of personal preference. Because schools are expected to serve the public, public opinion about what schools should accomplish is sampled through the use of various questionnaires that are commonly referred to as *needs assessments*. From these questionnaires lists of goals are stated that are general, inoffensive, and reflect majority opinion. The use of needs assessments leads parents to believe they have participated in establishing the goals of education. It is uncertain how responsive they expect the schools to be to these statements or, in fact, how responsive the schools are. Past the goal level, consensus is achieved and conflict avoided through a process that reduces the value questions built into any discussion about goals—such as, what should the schools be accomplishing?—into technical questions that have the appearance of value neutrality and objectivity. What should schools do? is changed to, How can it best be done? "How" questions can then be resolved by appeal to tradition or to the findings of analytical-empirical research. In either case there need not be thoughtful discussion of the explicit or implicit goals.

This process is mystifying because it is buried in the connections that are made between goal statements and the objectives used to guide instruction. Once the goals are stated, translating them into a form useful for guiding instruction is thought to be a simple matter of breaking down the larger ones into their constituent parts. As in a picture puzzle, each piece represents a specific objective that requires mastery. But goals intended to include something for everyone require more than analysis and translation to be useful for instruction. They require considerable definition or redefinition and reduction before they can be used in making decisions about classroom activities. In the process of making them concrete, the actual outcomes of schooling are revealed but not recognized or discussed as goals. This process is given a kind of simplicity by the belief that all worthwhile learning can be demonstrated behaviorally. A fundamental value of this outlook is that the range of human experience important for learning may be narrowed to what can be observed.

The broad goal statements we began with are gradually worked over until they become a list of desired behaviors that teachers are expected to facilitate and students to demonstrate. This reduction is assumed to be a translation of the abstract into the concrete with nothing lost or distorted. In fact not only are judgments involved in the initial decision to reduce values to behaviors, but they are also involved in the selection of those behaviors that are to be taken as proof of goal accomplishment. Obviously even if we accept the view that behavior is the most important indicator of learning—and no doubt it is an important one—not every behavioral indication of goal accomplishment can be included in the curriculum. Selecting and sorting must go on. We must ask, then, by what standards are such judgments to be made? One response is that certain behaviors are more likely to appear on standardized achievement tests because they represent what experts see as fundamental content. The tests are accepted as scientific instruments that measure learning, and since there is a seeming consensus about what behaviors are important — though this has not been publicly discussed—issues such as whether the student is competent, or whether the behaviors actually indicate "understanding" (80-percent mastery is a rather simplistic and peculiar indication of this) do not come up.

Already in this brief discussion, five educational assumptions representative of technocratic-mindedness have emerged:

1. Standardization of human experience is necessary for education to take place; students should learn the same things in the same sequence.
2. Goals are essentially matters of opinion.
3. The process of translating goals into classroom actions is a technical (value-free) process.
4. Conflict is disruptive and to be avoided.
5. All important learnings can be behaviorally demonstrated and objectively tested (quantified).

A sixth and powerful general assumption of this curriculum model is that to achieve efficiency — an unquestioned system value — control over the behavior of teachers and students must be increased. This is accomplished in a variety of ways, but perhaps the most potent is linking behavioral objectives to measurement instruments.

A brief description of the district's reading curriculum illustrates how the use of behavioral objectives increases control of the formal curriculum over what happens in the classroom, and how the initial purposes of education are lost in a thicket of technical procedures.

> In the goal-based educational management system reading is divided into six major subdivisions or strands — phonics, structure, vocabulary, comprehension, study skills, and affective reading. Within the strands, curriculum is stated in units of study (goal units) which follow a sequence or spiral scope from kindergarten through twelfth grade. A series of criterion-reference placement tests for each strand are [sic] provided to help the teacher identify the appropriate instructional level for each student. Pre- and post-tests are provided for each goal unit to assess what a student already knows about a particular goal unit and the student's progress in learning the content of the unit. Mastery tests check for learning retention and competency in relation to the district's graduation requirements.[2]

Because the objectives become test questions, they define needs and indicate the progress of learning. It is easy to see why the purpose of schooling for both teachers and students can become test passing.

A further indication of the importance of control is found in the language used to describe the curriculum. The reader undoubtedly noticed the jargony nature of the wording in the preceding quote. But take another look. Note its logic—how it seems that there is a natural movement from reading, to strands, to units, to tests, to student progress and mastery. Then note the level of control of teacher and student behavior implied in this presumably logical educational process.

Let us look more closely at the emphasis on control through a consideration of a unit entitled "In the Beginning," written for the eighth grade. The course goal is "The student is able to demonstrate an understanding of theories explaining the earth's origin and changes that have taken place."[3] Because the meaning of *demonstrate* is not clear, we might assume we are free to teach as we think best. Not so. The area of choice is quickly narrowed by the instructional objectives, of which there are six in this unit. The nature of the desired learning is indicated by the verb in each objective. For example, "The student is able to *identify* the most widely accepted theory explaining the earth's origin" (emphasis added).[4] What the students must do to show understanding is clear: Mark an answer on a test. Of the six objectives for the unit, three require students to identify, two require them to recognize, and one requires that they be able to classify information. In each case the objectives have been written for ease of measurement by a multiple choice test. These objectives do not require understanding but rather require the ability to remember. A typical test item is: "What is the most widely accepted theory explaining the earth's origin?" Four possible answers are given: (1) a large mass of rotating gas and dust solidified; (2) gas pulled from the sun solidified; (3) a comet collided with the sun; and (4) a black hole collided with the sun.[5] Students demonstrate understanding by selecting the correct answer, which indicates the type and level of knowing desired. They need not explain the theory or present reasons why it is preferred. Either of these ways of assessing understanding would be difficult if not impossible to standardize. They need only to identify from a presented list the most widely held theory.

We are not suggesting that all of the goal units, instructional objectives, and test questions focus only on memory. Rather we wish to stress that the nature of this approach to curriculum making tends to reduce what counts as knowing to maximize control over what will be learned. In short what is stressed by the formal curriculum is the less significant, though more efficiently measured, aspects of becoming educated.

In this outlook atomizing teaching and learning by breaking them into small bits is thought necessary and desirable. Visualize, for example, what the curriculum in reading means in concrete ways for a student attending school in this district for thirteen years. Remember we are discussing a complex human process of learning how to *understand* the expression of others through the medium of printed symbols. Pieces of mastered content somehow connect into mastery of goal units that add up to mastery of reading. Passing all of the tests at the 80-percent level therefore equals mastery of reading. One must ask if there is room for intuition, insight, that "aha!" experience many of us associate with understanding: "Now I see what the author means!" That the purpose is to help students learn to read can easily be lost because the identified parts of reading become the focus for testing and teaching.

This discussion of reading discloses yet another assumption: Educational experts must make the important decisions about teaching and learning. Experts are required because they understand the process of reading and because they produce the instruments for assessing student learning. While understanding the reading process may require expert knowledge, surely all students are capable of knowing what they can read. In this case an emphasis on evaluation obscures the fact that a test is not necessary to determine adequacy of student reading. In reading, as in many other skills, the act of doing is an indication of being able to do. The need for tests is an expression of a need for increased control by outsiders over what happens in the classroom rather than the need to inform the learner.

A latent implication of the role of the expert in this model of curriculum development is problematic for teachers. One would expect that because others make such important educational decisions that these same persons would be held accountable when their decisions go awry. This apparently is not the case. In the model the teacher stands between the student and the curriculum when systemic problems arise, such as how boring it is to be continually tested. Thus the teacher, rather than the persons who decided testing is so important, *takes* the brunt of student discontent. Though teachers might respond by saying it is not their doing, this does little to diffuse the problem. And if students do not pass the tests, most likely the activities selected by the teacher are seen as needing modification—not the objectives or the test questions. In either case because the creators of the system are distant they are invulnerable. By expressing their ideas in the form of a system, experts become holders of arcane knowledge to which mere teachers are not privileged. This occurs although many of the teachers were involved in creating parts of the curriculum.

This approach to curriculum making also holds that accountability is highly desirable. Although few would argue that we should not be accountable for our actions, the experts' contribution is secure from evaluation while they urge that the system "places accountability in proper perspective between student and teacher."[6] Certainly both teacher and student should accept responsibility for what occurs in the classroom, but they should also, one would think, have a say in what it is they are to be responsible for. The model effectively constrains the necessity for discussing the ends toward which they work.

The curriculum system, however, does not escape evaluation. Its effectiveness is determined by districtwide achievement test scores. The new curriculum works, according to the district, because the scores have improved. This method of determining success almost guarantees its attainment as it simultaneously confirms the value of controlling teachers and students by a standardized system. Better test results are a sure thing because the increased control over how students' spend their time means that their effort is focused on learning what is on the achievement tests. The curriculum does not ensure more learning, but as long as teachers cooperate, it does ensure narrowly focused learning and subsequently higher test scores.

To our first list of assumptions, we can now add six more:

1. To extend efficiency, greater control is needed over the actions of teachers and students.
2. Teaching and learning proceed best when the content is divided into small pieces and is sequenced according to the logic of the subject matter.
3. Teaching is the management of materials and persons and does not and should not include establishing educational aims.
4. There should be a separation and a specialization of educational functions; specifically, the important educational decisions should be made by experts.
5. Teachers and students should be held accountable to objectives developed by experts.
6. Student scores on multiple choice tests are the best indicator of effective teaching.

TEACHER TALK

Up to this point, we have examined the curriculum ideas that we see as indicators of technocratic-mindedness. We shall turn now to the talk of teachers in this system to see just how a positivistic approach to curriculum development reinforces technocratic-mindedness. So far we have been speaking only about the formal curriculum, but the following discussion shows how twenty interviewed teachers see the formal curriculum as well as the informal one—that is, what actually goes on.

The most salient technocratic aspects of the formal curriculum to come out of the interviews were (1) a pervasive faith in technological systems or, stated differently, in the desirability of standardizing human experience to realize efficiency; (2) belief in the necessity to separate and specialize educational functions; and (3) acceptance of the value of districtwide control over the curriculum.

Before considering how these points were expressed when teachers discussed their work, we will describe our data-gathering procedures. We used a semistructured interview with twenty volunteer teachers. They were each asked the same questions, and their responses were recorded on audiotape and transcribed. Our reasons for using interviews rather than a questionnaire were as follows. First, we wanted the teachers to provide some of the structure for their responses, which we hoped would indicate their perceptions, attitudes, and understandings. Second, an interview opens the possibility of asking clarifying and probing questions to help teachers share more complex and subtle meanings about their work. Our interviewees were identified by the school principals as teachers who understood and were effectively implementing the new curriculum. Successful teachers, we hoped, would provide something of an ideal view of the curriculum. Nevertheless, generalizations from our findings do not apply to the way all district teachers think about their work. Rather our reason for studying these specific teachers was to understand the influence of the context in which they work on how they think, talk, and probably act.

Each teacher was asked to respond to five statements and questions.

1. Describe how you use the Goal-Based Education Management System (GEMS) in your teaching.
2. What does GEMS allow you to do that you would otherwise not do?
3. What does GEMS require you to do that you would rather not do?

4. How does GEMS change the ways in which students spend their time?
5. Why do you think the school district has gone to the time and expense of developing a program such as GEMS?

A brief and general summary of the responses to the five questions follows. The typical response to the first question corresponded to the description in district literature. Teachers saw themselves using the curriculum the way it was designed to be used. In summarizing the responses to questions 2 and 3, which are the centrally important ones, we will merely indicate for now that the teachers appeared confused about the influence of the curriculum on their teaching. They seemed to have done little thinking about the possible limits or areas of freedom provided by GEMS. Interestingly, the responses to question 4 were brief and often focused on systems instead of students. Responses to the final question indicated that teachers saw the new curriculum as fulfilling a legitimate need to standardize in order to improve achievement test scores. The teachers generally felt satisfied with the new curriculum and thought that GEMS had improved their teaching. The powerful parts of the interviews reveal the extent to which technocratic-mindedness pervades their talk.

TEACHERS' CONCEPTION OF WORK

Faith in the power of technological systems to solve problems for humans has important implications for education. It indicates support of the basic proposition that the way to achieve progress in education is to carefully and progressively limit the arena within which human decision making is possible. Predictability is encouraged by limiting the possibility and impact of individual decision making. The implicit assumption is that human judgment is clearly inferior to the decision responses built into the structure of institutions. Only the judgments of a chosen few are to be honored while everyone else's are either denigrated or declared aberrant. This outlook is present in the large amount of talk urging the desirability of increased "uniformity," "standardization," and "control" in education.

It is important to note that while these teachers seem to accept considerable limitation on the range of their professional decision making as necessary and desirable, they have received something in return. They have traded a wide range of professional possibilities for security: If they follow the program, they have guaranteed results. Hence while their growth potential appears constrained, they generally feel positive about teaching and potent as teachers. Although understandable, given the pressures under which teachers work, this response is alienating and ultimately self-defeating. We will touch on this point later in this chapter.

The importance of standardization and uniformity is expressed in a variety of ways such as "I think you need programs just to standardize things" or "I've got a continuity I'm following." One teacher said, "You are seeing a consistency. You are seeing a kid who in sixth grade started here and eighth grade went to here. . . . We know *exactly* what the kid did in sixth. . . . [We] get a true three-year program." This situation is contrasted to that existing prior to the district's development of GEMS: "Before we had a districtwide approach or a school approach to something, that sixth grader might get one reading teacher who did this and the next year no consistency of what they had done previously." The logic of this last teacher's view is obvious. At the extreme it is an argument for a standardized national curriculum where, as the French once could boast, we would be able to tell what was being studied each moment of the school day in every classroom.

These teachers, like many of the others interviewed, seemed unable to imagine an alternative between the extremes of all teachers "doing their own thing" or of having complete standardization. What is generally desired is to know "exactly" what each student has had. It is questionable whether humans *need* such consistency or whether it is not a concern created by a technocratic system that requires an increasingly higher degree of order to function efficiently. These teachers seem to accept the dictates of a curriculum system such as GEMS in part because they assume there is a simple, direct link between behavior and inner experience and that behavior is what really counts in learning. Apparently they assume that having students do the same activity will mean that the experience of this activity—the learning—will be the same for each student. Common sense would indicate that we cannot control human beings so completely even if such control was desirable. Though the curriculum may be systematically organized, students' experience of it may be similar but never the same; as a result there will be a range of learning "outcomes." The faith that these teachers indicate in the power of a system to standardize learning seems to be justified only to a limited extent, but they choose to ignore the subjectivity of experience and to emphasize how a carefully planned system can produce predictability.

While the GEMS teachers seem to ignore the unique aspects of experience, they do focus on a part of human life that can be standardized. Though there is a private aspect to each person's experience, what teachers and students must do can be made uniform. The activity of both is carefully circumscribed by the curriculum. As one teacher commented: "Well, basically, I think it is just a system to organize what you do." Another teacher, one who wanted even greater control, commented, "If we are going to implement the program, then I think we should have a lot more guidelines rather than just materials. Here is what you do. We have workshops set aside for that, for credit but [they are] after school hours and everyone is tired." Yet another commented that she liked "the way [the curriculum is] outlined so I know supposedly what those students were taught when they were in the fourth-grade reading level, and what I need to teach on the fifth-grade reading level. Then I don't overstep my bounds and teach what they are going to learn on a sixth-grade reading level. To me the main advantage is the scope and sequence so I know exactly [there is that word again] what they've been taught and will be taught and what I'm supposed to teach them."

What these teachers can count on is not learning but rather that each student has *done* essentially the same things. Each has worked through the same activities and demonstrated the same behaviors as indication of the accomplishment of an identical set of instructional objectives.

In order to maintain this faith in systems, it is often necessary for these teachers to explain away problems that arise. By so doing they indicate the degree to which they share system values. Generally such problems are identified as technical in nature and therefore subject to correction by further or improved systematization. For example, one teacher complained about the diversity she is forced to recognize as a result of testing. Test scores are spread out, which produces problems in grouping students according to ability. Rather than seeing this problem as built into the system, she remarked, "Of course, that might be corrected by a different management system [one] not allowing the group to become so spread out." Another teacher recognized a problem because "at times students get tested out." But this problem is seen as primarily centering in the "readability of the material. The tests that are given on a third- or fourth-grade level, the readability is not third- or fourth-grade readabilty as far as I'm concerned. There's no way they can read the test even if they know the idea." Hence the problem is not with the heavy reliance upon testing but with the way in which the tests are written — a technical problem.

Besides defining problems as technical as a way of removing the problematic, a number of teachers also blamed themselves for system shortcomings. One stated, "If anything, where we have a hang up . . . must be [with] teachers." Others commented on how important it is to keep *other* teachers, particularly, first-year teachers, from doing anything they want. One teacher put it very clearly when she said that the system is a "safeguard" to make certain teachers do their job. Some even suggested that instructors need to be carefully controlled if they are to teach well. One teacher said, for example, that the curriculum system probably kept him from "just teaching things I like to teach or teaching things that strike my fancy." Yet another remarked, "It makes sure I don't leave parts out that I might not be interested in and dwell on other parts and makes certain I touch base with all of the materials, rather than stay with what I feel interested in." Another teacher, who lacked training and experience, commented appreciatively that it "gave me a starting point. It told me the goals that I need . . . what the kid at that level should be doing."

After reading the interviews, one gets the feeling that teachers cannot be trusted to teach what is important and that they probably cannot determine what is significant in the first place. Since the curriculum is presented in the form of an organized, complete, and obviously powerful system, it is as though it was created by nonhumans or superhumans rather than by other humans who might have their own particular and peculiar axes to grind. Teachers have reified the system and its objectives into something that transcends human beings and their abilities to make good judgments.

As indicated, this faith and the related lack of faith in human judgment include a belief in the ability of systems to equalize the performance of teachers. Only two of the twenty teachers interviewed talked about the importance of the teacher in implementing the curriculum. One stated, "Above all, you have to remember that it's the person who teaches it, not the program. So if you have the kind of personality that communicates and you're positive with kids you will do a good job." However, this teacher did not feel that many colleagues have the desired characteristics. "I think," she said, "you need programs just to standardize things and give everybody a basic—some people always do more than others . . . but there are people who do a super job and not get so involved with details and still get it over because of their personality." She seems to see the importance of personality in teaching, but such qualities are viewed as rare and not to be depended on. As a result she believes that standardization is necessary because the excellent teacher will still be excellent while the others will be forced to perform better. In any case there is a general belief that the only road to improvement in education is to move toward greater standardization, and that this can best be done through the development of more sophisticated educational systems. Human intelligence, insight, surprise, and wonder have no place in such programs except within the interstices of the school day—places which educationally do not matter.

The teacher who commented that she is concerned about keeping her instruction within "bounds" provides a good entry point for a more direct discussion of a topic touched on earlier. This is the acceptance of assumptions of the necessity and desirability of control and teachers' general blindness to its operation in their own professional lives. What we are referring to here goes far beyond the commonplace observation that a certain level of control is needed to keep any class working and learning. This is, of course, obvious. What these teachers emphasize is that system control is an essential condition for good education. This teacher's concern for staying within bounds is an important and shared indication of the commitment. She does not see that it is even a problem; instead it is viewed as a necessary and proper part of being a good "team player." She fails to recognize that to stay within bounds—to make certain that fifth graders only learn what they are supposed to as fifth graders and not get into sixth-grade content (whatever that is!)—is to say that it is necessary to place arbitrary limits on human growth in order to maintain what one teacher called a "smoother education."

Teachers accept this assumption ambiguously and inconsistently. According to one teacher, "It doesn't keep you from doing things and it doesn't require you to do things either. . . . If you are going to be involved with the program, then of course you have certain things you need to do. But it requires you to teach materials that are going to accomplish a particular goal." Her ambiguity makes it possible for the assumption to continue unchallenged. Another teacher commented that the system is "great" but then went on to say that it provides her "little" freedom because she is always "fighting to get the concepts . . . taught" and if she fails, "it puts the child further behind. So I think in GEMS you have to do it. Have to commit yourself."

One explanation of this ambiguity and inconsistency is that a person does not consciously feel controlled by natural forces. We know that gravity, for instance, controls much of what we do, but there is no conscious feeling of control because gravity is a natural—built in—phenomenon. As we have argued above, a system in a technocratic context is also seen as natural. The control is not felt as control—as being forced to do something. There is a general insensitivity to the hidden or latent functions of the system that compel or entice desired behavior, and even when these functions are seen, they are accepted as unavoidable. For instance, one teacher commented on how important it is to get her name on the computer printout. When questioned, she revealed that no one had ever told her she had to do this. She just knew it had to be done and accepted it. Another teacher expressed the same kind of ambivalence in this way: "Lots of teachers think they don't want to do GEMS because they are telling me how to teach. I don't see it as that at all. It's just kind of a way of saying this is what should be taught in the third grade." For this teacher and for almost all of her colleagues, teaching has nothing to do with determining what will be taught. It is natural and proper that others do this. By so defining teaching they have successfully set aside what might have been a problematic situation. For these teachers the system does and it does not control; it does and it does not require them to do anything. What control they do see is taken as natural and unavoidable. They do not see any alternatives. We did not find in the interviews teachers who felt inappropriately controlled by the curriculum though in some instances some small amount of frustration was expressed relating to what they had to do in order to make things run smoothly. In general this frustration centered on the uses of time.

Teachers also accepted the view that to attain efficiency it is necessary and natural for functions to be separated and specialized. Before exploring this characteristic, we should make a general comment about the talk, or rather the lack of talk, of a normative kind found in our interviews. For the most part, the teachers did not raise questions about the values, the goals, or aims toward which they work. They accepted the goals presented to them without question as the proper aims of education. Thus we can infer that system values and the values held by these teachers are generally congruent. And while this appears to be the case, one cannot help being struck by the abundance of contradictions, as those relating to control, within teachers' thinking about their work. It appears that they accept system values as desirable or at least as inevitable expressions of modern living, in part because they see no reason to question—or perhaps, possibility of doing so. There is so little normative talk because they assume there is only one way of seeing the world, and yet they constantly must account, as we have seen, for situations with implications contrary to this view.

Because teachers do not question, it is clear students learn to follow their example. Teachers instruct, and students do what they are told and, presumably, thereby learn. One teacher expressed relief that her students did not question: "Something I tried this year that I found very interesting is when we began GEMS goals, I would tell students, 'here's what we want to do. . . . ' Because I was able to tell them exactly what I wanted in terms of goals, what my goal was for them, they had a clearer purpose in where they were going. I didn't get questions like, 'Why are we doing this?' They knew why they were doing it. . . . Students feel like they have a direction. . . . That's a security thing for them." But one must ask, whose meaning do they have? Their own or someone else's? The same questions can be asked of the teachers.

The desirability of separating and specializing functions is related to the acceptance of several technocratic values, specifically those associated with a production understanding of efficiency. In this particular pattern of curriculum development, separation and specialization of functions emerges gradually and presumably naturally (efficiency demands it). Most important to this development is teachers' acceptance of the view that they ought not to be involved in establishing goals even though at one time in the program's development some teachers were in fact very involved. They tend to reify goals, in part because they assume them to be products of individuals possessing particular expertise and in part because there has been a highly visible payoff that confirms the wisdom of this separation. One teacher describes the payoff in this way: "What we've been able to accomplish . . . is that our scores have gone up just by simply having an organized program. I don't believe we teach for the Iowa [the Iowa Test of Basic Skills]. I think we teach GEMS and [high Iowa test scores have] just been a nice side bonus." As a side note, it is worth commenting on this teacher's failure to see that it is no accident that scores on the Iowa test have increased. One must ask if it is conceivable that a school district would choose to use a test that did not confirm the wisdom and worth of a considerable investment in a particular curriculum program. In any case the job of teachers is taken to be that of working toward goals established by others, which means they are managers of materials and persons. In addition, for these teachers, curriculum development has become reduced to sorting and labeling of materials according to how they fit into a particular predetermined set of objectives. A similar process, the process of sorting and of labeling young people, is accomplished for teachers by the testing feedback system.

In accepting that others should establish their goals, the teachers generally do not see that their teaching is heavily influenced by the prescription of content and skill objectives. Yet as we say in our discussion of control, they do occasionally mention examples of this influence that they find somewhat irritating. They are not troubled more because they have accepted the view that their function is primarily one of instruction. Instruction does not include deciding what will be taught; this is better done by others.

It is in the selection of means that these teachers find their professional importance. This ability gives them a sense of potency that carries with it a certain sense of freedom; they have a clear statement of purposes along with the possibility of varying teaching methods. Yet teachers generally overemphasize the range of choice involved in selecting or creating teaching methods. In particular, a disregard for how objectives are produced, stated, and verified constricts the range of instructional options. Teachers do not seem aware, for example, that when objectives are stated in behavioral or performance form for testing, the students must be given practice in the desired behavior. When objectives are stated in terms of specific content mastery, students require some kind of drill in order to be able to ensure repetition of the desired information in a testing situation. Their comments show lack of awareness of limited instructional options. One teacher commented, for instance, that "GEMS just gave me guidelines on what I should teach. Then I could put my own method [in]." For her, ends are clearly separated from means. Another teacher felt that GEMS provides "basically just organization." In this process what the students value is often most likely to be lost. As one teacher put it, "I had to almost feed them the test in order for them to pass it. The kids would say, 'When are we going to read in reading? It's really neat to read.'"

We can only assume that the feeling of freedom and potency expressed by most of these teachers is something of a distortion. Yet this is perhaps too harsh a judgment. The teachers did feel increased potency because the curriculum guide and the heavy use of testing establish clear expectations that they can fulfill. Furthermore, the technocratic emphasis on "tangible proof" of the success of a given treatment is difficult to avoid. In short a rise in test scores does give a certain sense of satisfaction often lacking in many teaching situations, and test passing *is* taken as *the* proof of learning. As one teacher said, "I know if I'm proceeding through GEMS. I don't have to tailor a particular thing to review kids for the Iowa test. I feel like if they're progressing through GEMS, the Iowa test is going to take care of itself and doesn't give me a lot of worry." Not having to worry—

securing a sense of certainty — also adds to a feeling of freedom and potency.

These teachers face a situation that is clearly paradoxical. On one hand, they have accepted a set of assumptions built into the curriculum model that, among other things, requires them to work ever harder to produce conditions of greater control and efficiency. These assumptions have led them to accept a narrow role of teacher as manager/clerk that does not include the power to establish the ends toward which they will work. On the other hand, the harder they work in the spirit of a developing professionalism, the less personal investment and involvement they will have in their own education and that of their pupils. This is expressed clearly in terms of the denigration of human judgment that is built into the system. It is also seen in the way interviewees speak about needs and about individualizing. Needs are seen as determined by the system—system-identified "lacks"—while individualizing has little to do with the individual. In fact, in reference to individualization, it is not necessary for a teacher to speak with the student who is being individualized—though fortunately they do. The harder teachers work within this kind of curriculum, the less humane their teaching becomes. The situation is produced by a system that necessitates the separation of ends from means and produces a false sense of potency in those who serve the ends established by others.

The crux of the problem for teachers interested in developing critical-mindedness is for them to recognize that their professional/personal interests are not served by the system. That is, they must question the belief that their goals are the same as the goals established for them. As long as this perception remains, the development of a genuine sense of potency that might affect the quality of life in the classrooms will be blunted. The technical kind of potency teachers are encouraged to develop limits awareness of the contradictions that frequently occur between system values and personal ones. Such contradictions, surely, are experienced as frustration by the teacher who always feels compelled "to stay within bounds." As shown, "to stay within bounds" is to accept arbitrary and destructive limits on human growth.

THE TECHNOCRATIC CURRICULUM AND ALIENATION

In the *Economic and Philosophic Manuscripts*, Karl Marx discusses various features of alienation or estrangement that are useful categories for examining teachers' thinking and attitudes. We will use these categories by way of summarizing and giving focus to our discussion. Among the features Marx identifies are: (1) estrangement of the worker from the product of his labor, (2) estrangement from the act of production, (3) estrangement from one's natural being, and (4) estrangement from other men. We will discuss each of these features as it appears in the interviews and suggest ways of talking that would indicate movement *away* from alienation.

Within a technological society, student learning is commonly viewed as the product of teacher labor. The way teachers talk about learning and content can be taken as an indicator of alienation or movement away from alienation. We would expect teachers moving away from alienation to talk in ways suggesting that they (1) see learning as dynamic and interactive, (2) involve students in establishing goals, and (3) see subject areas as tools for solving human problems.

The teachers we interviewed showed few if any of these characteristics. Actually, the opposite seemed to be the general rule. They did not talk about learning in ways that showed interest, understanding, or introspection into the complexity of coming to know. It was evident that interviewees saw their role as managing materials to acquire predetermined outcomes rather than as facilitating learning through interaction involving problem posing, exploration, questioning, and the like. We saw no indication that they viewed content and skills as tools for solving human problems; again, the opposite was true. Subjects and skills were seen as static things, as ends in themselves to be mastered for reasons outside of human interaction.

In terms of Marx's second category, the teachers' act of production involves the processes of teaching: planning and implementing lessons. We would expect teachers moving away from alienation to talk in ways demonstrating (1) active involvement in establishing (and questioning) educational goals, (2) that they were students of teaching, and (3) a willingness to change plans according to student needs.

We have discussed the lack of normative talk on the part of teachers; the teachers did not think about aims. Another factor missing from the interviews was talk suggesting that teachers were students of the teaching-learning process. Although experienced teachers, the interviewees seemed to lack a developed understanding of teaching, less than what might be anticipated from experienced teachers. We concluded that the teachers had as a result of increasing alienation lost much of their interest in their work — interest of the kind that compels craftsmen to further develop their craft. As Marx states, the estranged worker, "does not develop freely his physical and mental energy . . . and ruins his mind." Thus work (teaching in this case) is a required activity that one does not commit oneself to: "As soon as no physical or other compulsion exists it is shunned like the plague." [7]

The nature of teachers' relationships to their natural or species being, Marx's third category, is seen in how they view human nature and learning. That is, what do teachers take as the essential characteristics of humans? We would expect teachers moving away from alienation to (1) value education as an end in itself rather than as a means to something else; (2) show concern for questions of fairness and right in the classroom; (3) recognize and honor human curiosity and creativity in its many manifestations; and (4) see human differences as enriching life.

The interviews show the opposite. There was no talk of student rights. Students were expected to do what others saw as important. Human differences were a source of annoyance rather than a quality to be valued. In addition, talk about student curiosity was absent from the interviews. Creativity was seen as a source of disruption to be avoided through system control.

Teaching is obviously an interactive affair: Teachers work with people. An important indication of alienation or movement away from alienation is found in teachers' relationships to students and colleagues. We would expect teachers moving away from alienation to (1) view other teachers' problems with understanding and empathy, (2) enjoy professional relationships, (3) seek opportunities to share professional and personal understandings with students and colleagues, (4) provide opportunities for interaction and free discussion in the classroom, and (5) stress the affective aspects of education.

The lack of trust between teachers and lack of faith in their colleagues to work responsibly is a particularly distressing part of the interviews. The interaction among teachers seemed minimal and focused on the managerial aspects of instruction. The induction of new teachers was described as a process of showing them how to fit rather than a dialogue from which both the experienced and the neophyte could learn. In addition the affective aspect of education, an important indicator of valuing others, was mostly ignored.

The GEMS teachers did talk like the estranged or alienated persons described by Marx. Undoubtedly many factors have produced this condition, but in our view the most powerful is the presence of a technocratic view of education. To work with a curriculum such as GEMS and respond in other than alienated ways would be difficult—although not impossible. We have demonstrated how teachers who were moving away from alienation would talk because it raises the question of what is worth thinking about and doing when one lives and works within a technocratic system. Through reason and dialogue, groups of teachers can come to understand the conditions under which they work; through collective effort, they can make changes that will aid in the gradual emancipation of themselves and their students. It is blind acceptance that alienates us from our species being, and only through critical questioning, conversation, and action can we move to make ourselves and others more free. The pervasiveness of technocratic-mindedness makes the task of personal emancipation difficult but not impossible. Further, it is only through making this effort that we can move away from alienation and in the direction of more complete human living.

Chapter 3

Learning to Labor

A formal curriculum and the talk of teachers indicate the domination of technocratic-mindedness, but they may say little about actual school practices or about the quality of school life. What is life like within an elementary school committed to a highly rationalized curriculum form? And, importantly, what is learned from living such a life? To address these questions, we selected for study a school strongly committed to using Individually Guided Education (IGE), a program grounded in the assumptions about schooling discussed in the preceding chapter. We will call the school Flowing Brook.

IGE was developed under the direction of Herbert J. Klausmeier, a prominent educational psychologist at the University of Wisconsin Research and Development Center for Cognitive Learning, and it has been widely adopted in schools throughout the United States. According to Klausmeier, IGE "is a comprehensive alternative . . . it represents a change of great magnitude."[1] This claim and the wide adoption of the program encouraged our study.

GEMS and IGE are not identical programs. There are differences in how and where curriculum decisions are made. However, they share a technical approach to education. They have the same major ingredients in different packaging. This similarity is evident when their instructional models are compared. The IGE model is shown as model 2. While this model contains more detail than the GEMS model and adds two steps (step 2 and step 4), the programs are fundamentally the same. Note, for instance, that both emphasize the careful sequencing of precisely stated and measurable objectives and stress testing. Like all such programs, IGE is highly rationalized and systematized, expressing a dominating interest in control.

MODEL 2. *IGE Instructional Model*

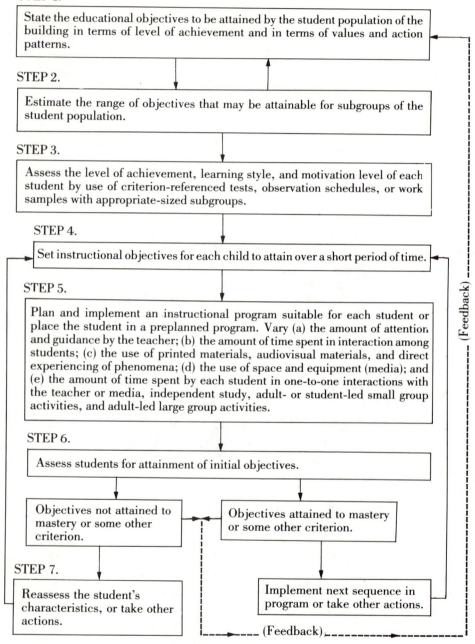

STEP 1.

State the educational objectives to be attained by the student population of the building in terms of level of achievement and in terms of values and action patterns.

STEP 2.

Estimate the range of objectives that may be attainable for subgroups of the student population.

STEP 3.

Assess the level of achievement, learning style, and motivation level of each student by use of criterion-referenced tests, observation schedules, or work samples with appropriate-sized subgroups.

STEP 4.

Set instructional objectives for each child to attain over a short period of time.

STEP 5.

Plan and implement an instructional program suitable for each student or place the student in a preplanned program. Vary (a) the amount of attention and guidance by the teacher; (b) the amount of time spent in interaction among students; (c) the use of printed materials, audiovisual materials, and direct experiencing of phenomena; (d) the use of space and equipment (media); and (e) the amount of time spent by each student in one-to-one interactions with the teacher or media, independent study, adult- or student-led small group activities, and adult-led large group activities.

STEP 6.

Assess students for attainment of initial objectives.

Objectives not attained to mastery or some other criterion.

Objectives attained to mastery or some other criterion.

STEP 7.

Reassess the student's characteristics, or take other actions.

Implement next sequence in program or take other actions.

(Feedback)

(Feedback)

Source: H.J. Klausmeier, "Origin and Overview of IGE," in *Individually Guided Elementary Education: Concepts and Practices*, ed. H.J. Klausmeier, R. Rossmiller, and M. Saily (New York: Academic Press, 1977).

We studied Flowing Brook through observations and informal conversations with those involved: the principal, teachers, students, and staff
members such as the custodian. We each visited the school several times,
took notes on what we saw, and then discussed our findings with each
other. We tried to grasp the quality of school life in Flowing Brook by
attending to what teachers and students did and what students appeared to
be learning. After spending considerable time there, we visited a different
IGE school to see if what we had seen and heard at Flowing Brook was in
fact representative. It was. Though we observed some differences between
the two schools, they appeared to be merely surface differences.

We begin by describing how Flowing Brook appears to the casual
observer. We then examine in some detail the pervasive qualities and
characteristics of life within the school. Finally we consider how a peculiar
use of language and a particular strategy for educational research promotes
and legitimates the schooling practices we observed.

A TYPICAL DAY AT FLOWING BROOK

Flowing Brook is a suburban elementary school (K–6), surrounded
by neat, single-family houses and quiet curving streets. The lawns are well
kept, the trees young, and the feeling is middle-class America. Externally, the school looks like most contemporary public buildings. Inside,
however, it departs from standard format. The building is essentially one
huge, carpeted wall-less classroom. The ceiling is low and the windows are
few, features that accentuate its sense of isolation from the world outside.
Within that large space, teachers have used the material of the school—
shelves, filing cabinets, portable chalkboards — to create boundaries
marking individual classroom areas. Each teaching area also has its own
lighting system that is on when children are present and off when they are
gone, affording a curious but pleasant checkerboard effect of dark and
light intervals throughout the school at certain times of the day.

The children of Flowing Brook appear clean, well dressed, neat, and
mannerly, just like the surrounding houses and yards. To the observer they
are polite, occasionally venturing a question, often beaming a shy smile.
Their faces radiate trust and optimism; surely, one feels, these children
will have abundant opportunities to develop their diverse and wonderful
potentials.

The day begins with first and second graders clustered on the carpet listening to their teachers review the day's activities. The atmosphere is pleasant but businesslike; all voices are subdued, and all behavior seems purposeful. Show and Tell starts things rolling for the youngsters. The other grades, too, prepare for their work by discussing immediate plans and leftover problems. The daily litany's persistent message is clear (but not loud): "Get your work done."

About 9:15 A.M., pupils throughout the school move to groups for reading and language arts. Pupils and teachers at Flowing Brook are divided into three teams according to the age (grade level) of the children: first and second grade, third and fourth grade, and fifth and sixth grade. The number of teachers in each team depends on the number of children, but generally there are six teachers in each team including one who serves as a team leader. During the skill subjects—reading, language, mathematics—the children are grouped for instruction according to their ability relative to the others in that subject. Thus during reading, for example, those children within a team who are the "best" readers go to one teacher, the next best to another, and so on until all the children in each team are sorted into six ability groups. During the course of the day, a child is typically taught by two or three different teachers. The grouping pattern narrows the range of student variation within a class but increases the number of children a teacher must work with each day.

The children's day is spent primarily doing paper-and-pencil tasks from a workbook or worksheet. The teacher explains the day's assignments, and the students complete them at their desks. Most of the teachers divide their classes into subgroups so that while one group gets assignments and explanations of what is to be done, the other groups are working on assigned tasks. When students finish, they either hand their papers in, quietly line up at the teacher's desk for correction, or meet with the teacher as a group for correction. The general pattern of the morning is one of teachers explaining how to do assignments and correcting completed work while students do the assignments and have them checked off. It is a telling experience to stand in one of the unlighted areas and look out and see every student in almost every class doing the same thing: sitting, head bent over desk, working. The students are not the only ones who sit and work. The same panoramic view reveals almost every teacher sitting, head bent over desk, correcting papers. Our impression is that much of the students' and teachers' day is spent in this way.

Recess comes as a welcome break from the day's work. Recess is the students' own time: a time to behave like children. They kick and chase balls, jump rope, scream, laugh, and wrestle. Teachers watch the children at recess but only to make certain no one is hurt.

An important activity in the school lives of these children marks the beginning and end of recess; it is lining up. Lining up pervades life in Flowing Brook, and the children become very good at it and are rewarded for it. Whenever classes or groups go anywhere, even just thirty feet from one classroom area to another, they go in lines two abreast. Teachers lead the lines; students follow, quietly resigned.

Schoolwork from morning recess until lunch is essentially more of the same. Most students continue working on reading although a few teams move into mathematics. Math follows much the same pattern as reading. The teacher explains and in some cases demonstrates how to do problems, gives workbook assignments, helps those having difficulty, then corrects and records finished work. The students do their part by listening and working as directed. On our morning visits, we were always surprised at just how quiet a building full of children could be and at how long children can work at their desks without protest or engaging in much disruptive behavior.

Afternoons at Flowing Brook are somewhat less structured than mornings. The building is less quiet, and the range of activities expands. Students go to music, held in a special room, and study science and social studies by doing projects and textbook readings. They also see films and have physical education. Some art instruction goes on in the afternoons, but generally it is of the kind where the teacher directs the students in following a pattern to produce a specific object. For example, during our visits in the autumn and early winter, art served the function of decorating the building for various holidays. All of the children in a class made nearly identical colored-paper turkeys for Thanksgiving. For Halloween orange paper pumpkins were made by the younger classes, and nearly identical Santas reigned over the Christmas season. These were hung from the walls and ceilings. Though the color added much to the school environment, perhaps it is a misnomer to call these products "artwork." We will discuss this topic in the following chapter.

School ends much as it begins: quietly and in an orderly manner. The children leave the building without haste, talking in normal voices. As they walk out of the building, these young people seem much like wage earners who have finished yet another day of work. The real day begins when school is over. But another day of work always awaits.

In summary Flowing Brook is in many ways a successful school; successful, that is, in teaching children the basic skills of reading, the mechanics of language, arithmetic processes, and the elementary facts and concepts of social studies and science. It is also profoundly successful in teaching children to be obedient to persons in authority, to work consistently on assigned tasks in order to receive external rewards, and to confine their personal and social lives to the times they are outside the working place—to recess and before and after school. Put a bit differently, the most powerful learnings do not appear to be those concerned with the basic skills of literacy or certain ideas from the physical and social sciences but rather those that reinforce the values embedded in the preunderstanding. The structure of schooling at Flowing Brook presses home two crucial lessons. It teaches children to see as natural and right a very limited way of approaching learning, and it imbues them with a particularly restricted sense of legitimate power relationships for any place of work. How this is accomplished is the subject for discussion in the next section.

BECOMING A GOOD WORKER

The visitor entering Flowing Brook is struck by the orderliness of the school. Everything, including the student, is in place. Students move from class to class efficiently. There is little unnecessary talking or apparent wasted effort. Movement within the school is characterized by ease and certainty. Students know where they belong and what they are supposed to be doing. The pervasive message is the importance of orderly and unquestioning compliance to procedures that increase efficiency.

Achieving such a high degree of order is no small accomplishment; it requires commitment of the entire faculty and support from parents. The first day of school for new students begins their induction into the institutional role they are expected to play. In a short while they learn what is appropriate behavior and adjust accordingly; gradually almost complete conformity is achieved. This effort is so successful that teachers report with pride that they do not have discipline problems.

The commitment to achieving orderliness is expressed in a variety of ways throughout the program. One central emphasis, for example, is upon cooperation. Teachers and students cooperate with one another to maintain the desired learning environment. This does not mean, however, that students are encouraged to work together on school tasks although they sometimes do. Rather cooperation as conformity to specifically defined roles is urged. The language is that of cooperation, of helping one another, but the reality is that of conformity and obedience. Students demonstrate their cooperation by conforming to system imperatives; they do what they are told. To cooperate, then, for students is paradoxically to accept as inappropriate the desire to cooperate in the sense of "explore with" or "interact with" other students.

Teachers are not excused from this paradox. For them cooperation also means conformity but in a slightly different and more complex sense. The complexity derives from the bureaucratic decision-making structure of IGE. This involves teachers in curriculum decision making through participation in a team whose leader serves on the Instructional Improvement Council (IIC) chaired by the principal. Teaming spreads out the responsibility for failure and success but calls for a high degree of coordination. Each member of the team must plan her curriculum and teach in a way that is specifically and carefully related to the work of the other team members. The team leader must encourage her team to conform to the general pattern followed by other teams in the school. The possibility of expressing individuality is thus narrowed, and the pressure for conformity increased. A functionalist view of teaching prevails; there are certain team tasks that must be performed for the program to run as the designers intended. Efficiency demands that the lines of authority and responsibility be clear and definite, and cooperation for the individual teacher means accepting necessary limitations on her activity. The aim of the teacher is to make certain her classes are a smoothly operating part of the whole. She therefore must continually ask whether she is meeting the expectations of others. Cooperation, is, indeed, conformity.

Team success is judged by achievement test scores and on how smoothly the team runs. Hence conflict, even when potentially growth producing, is avoided. Tension within a team arouses suspicion in other teams that something is amiss, that someone is not doing her job properly. Such suspicion is an important stimulus for making certain that problems do not become significant, thereby calling unwanted attention to the team. So powerful is the sense of being watched that there is virtually a tyranny of the environment in Flowing Brook. Teaming, team leaders, open physical space, and use of various instructional programs all serve to establish a carefully defined role to which all teachers conform rather willingly; they cooperate for the good of the program. Though not as evident, teachers also cooperate in a more positive sense. For example, we observed two of the intermediate grade teachers working together on a science unit. They planned and divided responsibilities according to their knowledge and skills. It is not that cooperation of the sharing and helping sort does not occur at Flowing Brook, but rather that the emphasis on conformity and smoothness of operation tends to discourage more than encourage such mutuality.

Orderliness is not explicitly stated as a goal or desired outcome of an IGE program, but in practice it becomes the most easily available and important evidence of teacher and program success. The ability of a teacher to keep her charges working quietly is the most visible part of the teaching repertoire and of most importance to the work of other teachers in the team. One teacher in a team whose class is disruptive makes the work of the other teachers more difficult. Thus colleagues justly appreciate the teacher who maintains a high level of order. Certainly a degree of orderliness and respect is necessary in any school, but when orderliness supersedes more significant goals of education, then it becomes a final end rather than a condition conducive to learning. By a change of emphasis, qualities that should be valued only when they enhance learning become more important than any other habits or ideas that might be learned. An example of this reversal of priorities comes from our observation of Jacob S., a second-grade student (Jacob S. is a fictitious name).

> *9:50*—Jacob has a worksheet in front of him that he should be working on. He seems to be doodling. He flips his pencil out into the darkened open space in front of his desk. It is a dead zone. I expected him to go and get it, but he didn't pay any attention to it.

> *9:57*—Jacob stands up and wanders over to the teacher [and] saunters back. I wonder if he feels compelled to ask the teacher if he can get his pencil. No, he doesn't seem to care one way or the other. He sits at his desk and quietly talks to himself—while talking he balances the front legs of his chair on his feet.

> *10:05*—He stands up and moves his chair around. The teacher has left her desk and is now working with a small reading group. He sits down, then stands up and wanders over to the teacher. He speaks to her, picks up another sheet, and walks back to his desk.

> *10:06*—He checks to see if the teacher is watching and then gets his pencil. He sits back down and begins to use his desk as a drum, a muffled, almost silent drum. He sneaks over to a neighbor for a quick visit, a matter of a couple of seconds—the teacher is busy and doesn't notice.

> *10:10*—He fiddles around with his worksheets something like the way a child plays with food that is distasteful but at some point must be

consumed. He begins to make train noises as he moves his pencil around his sheets.

10:15 — Still fidgeting. Buzzer goes off indicating recess. While he was away I went to his desk and noticed that he hadn't made a single mark on his worksheets. At recess he kicks a partially flat ball and chases it around the playground.

10:30 — Kids are lining up to return from recess. The buzzer sounds, and there is an unbelievable explosion of energy from deep within the kids as though they have been simultaneously startled by something quite frightening. (There was something primal about this explosion of energy. When it happened some kids were lining up in an informal way still bouncing balls and talking vigorously. Others were running around the playground. Almost everybody screamed. It was as if by reflex response to the buzzer; their bodies knew that it was time to release one last burst of energy before getting back to quiet work.)

10:37 — Jacob is in his seat fiddling. He taps with the eraser end of his pencil on the worksheet while gazing down on it. I cannot hear his taps.

10:43 — He wanders once again up to the teacher—she doesn't say a word to him. She points to something on his paper with her pencil.

10:45 — Buzzer. Jacob is coloring the bottom half of his worksheet with a little girl. He is obviously very pleased. She goes back to her seat.

10:51 — Jacob stands up, checks to see if the teacher is looking, and goes over to the girl who colored with him. They are supposed to be reading quietly. He returns. Across the aisle they engage in a rapid sharing of book pictures and a quick and quiet smile.

Jacob's actions show that he has learned two important facts of school life. He has learned to gauge the exact amount of orderliness he must conform to, and he has learned that he can escape from the paper-and-pencil work if he does it without disrupting others. The teacher does not notice Jacob because Jacob is quiet. The chugging sounds he made as his pencil-train moved around his worksheet did not reach into another child's space. He did little disrupting though he did have a brief and mutually enjoyable encounter with the student who colored with him. He did not, in short, do anything that interfered with the efficient flow of the day's activities. Clearly it was less important for him to finish the assigned work than it was to maintain his unobtrusiveness.

Jacob serves as an example of how orderliness and obedience are more important than education, and how the smooth operation of the system is paramount. Such an emphasis ensures that some students will fail. But the vast majority of students at Flowing Brook are obedient. Not only are they quiet, but they are doing the assigned work; they keep their noses in their books and produce as they are told without the slightest indication of resistance. These students are succeeding in school. But the question is, what are they learning?

Becoming a good worker, or at least looking like one, is highly prized in Flowing Brook. Most of the students develop good worker habits quickly. Rewards abound for such behavior. Good workers are, for instance, allowed to participate in selected art activities before their less motivated classmates. Praise is given freely to students who follow directions precisely and promptly. Those who finish their work within the allotted time are given recognition; they have learned that neither too much nor too little time should be spent on any one assignment. Disapproval plays its part as well. For example, attention is called to those students who do not line up quickly and quietly to go to lunch. The other students, the good workers, bring pressure to bear on the uncooperative because they understand that a delay in getting to lunch means less time at recess.

Learning to be a good worker means learning to be orderly, obedient, and passive. For this the children receive praise. There are other rewards in addition to praise. Good workers learn the basic skills; they spend time in carefully sequenced programs learning to decode symbols into sounds, to read a passage and answer questions about what it contains, to solve basic arithmetic problems, and to spell many words—certainly important achievements. But the school does not arouse authentic expressions of the desire to find out and to know why. There is tacit acknowledgment that in order for a systematic program to work efficiently, it cannot be grounded on the unsystematic feelings and intellectual interest of human beings. The systematic program is constructed on the metaphor of the machine, and those aspects of being human that do not fit with this metaphor are discouraged.

Human curiosity is truncated. Thus while children become more controllable, they also become progressively less capable of autonomy. They are educated for followership. Perhaps this assessment appears harsh. Albeit, a look at other aspects of Flowing Brook, and how its emphasis on conformity and efficiency restricts the range of emotional and intellectual expression, adds support to our thesis that the technocratic curriculum enables particular outcomes while limiting the possibility that schooling will lead to increased autonomy.

BENDING THE TWIG

The pleasantness of Flowing Brook makes it easy to forget that in general, learning involves overcoming obstacles, what Paulo Freire calls "limit situations."[2] Engaging our limits, whether in the ability to do calculus problems or to make meaning out of the sentence "See Dick run," involves us intellectually and emotionally. This is particularly the case when the obstacle to be overcome is taken as personally significant. When we get involved in learning, we feel tension, frustration, and excitement. We daydream. We wonder. We laugh and get excited. And perhaps, on occasion, we even feel joy.

For the young students in any elementary school, learning is only partially associated with those feelings. For them what is significant to learn and what is significant about learning are in large measure determined by adults who use a variety of techniques to ensure students' acceptance. Emotional involvement in learning for students is only partially associated with learning per se. It is also associated with the relationship the student has with the teacher. Hence the tension, for example, often felt when attempting to learn is overlaid with the fear that failure to learn might result in personal rejection. Children's need for acceptance requires them to learn what is presented and to do it in ways that will ensure their standing with the teacher and class.

While this is the case, it need not mean that learning is in itself unimportant. Presumably what is important for the young to learn is selected. But there is more here than simply learning the content presented. Students are often required not only to learn *what* the teachers want but also *how* the teachers want it learned. Students are expected to learn in the manner prescribed. That is, success for students in Flowing Brook requires that they learn to contain their expressions of emotion and intellect. Emotional expression is restricted by constant pressure to be orderly and quiet while time and subject matter constraints virtually preclude the play of intellect and its wider expression.

Let us be clear. We are not urging that students be permitted to do or say anything they want in schools. Obviously participation in a group activity necessitates some limitations on personal freedom. What strikes us about Flowing Brook is not so much that limitations are present but the degree and nature of the limitations themselves. We shall discuss these limitations by considering the quality of emotional life for students in Flowing Brook.

In our observations we witnessed only one occasion of total class laughter. There was little laughter that arose from personal encounters between individual teachers and students. We also witnessed only isolated instances of anger and frustration. Teachers did get upset with individual students on occasion, but this was most often the modulated irritation of adults who must supervise large groups of students in settings where quiet is important. In short there was a striking absence of either extreme — the spontaneous laugh or the emotional force of honestly felt anger or frustration. But it was pleasant, too pleasant.

The narrowing of the range of emotional expression was indicated forcefully in the tone of many teachers' voices. We are all aware of the hollowness and impersonal quality of the voices we encounter at the checkstand or over the phone when we call about our bank balance. We expect a businesslike quality in these voices. It does not disturb us because we recognize that we have little if any personal connection to this other voice. The exchange that takes place is between roles, not between feeling and caring persons. When we break off, we receive a polite but habitual "thank you" or "have a nice day," and we go about our activities as though the exchange had never taken place. This pleasant but impersonal *tone* characterized many of the interactions we saw in Flowing Brook. Whether the teachers were praising, reprimanding, or explaining, their voices sounded much the same.

As a result of this impersonal quality, there was frequent incongruity between tone and message. It was most apparent when teachers praised students. Although the words were those of appreciation and respect, the message was often one of disinterested control. It also made those few instances of genuine emotion stand out. This is illustrated from our observations:

"What instruction did Mrs. Bradley. . . . ?" Teacher with book on [her] knees, apparently asking questions listed in the teacher's manual. "What words did Stanley know?"

Her voice does not change in tone—no emotion at all. [She] gives directions and asks questions in the same tone, a monotone. "Why did William begin to worry?"

Across the way a contrast — "If you don't knock that off, I'm going to knock your head off!" A teacher with a voice!

The monotone continues. The rest of her class is doing seat work. The assignment is on the board. "Very good," she says, in the same voice.

The point is that teaching in Flowing Brook is more an impersonal function of curriculum management than an expression of human concern and understanding. Emotion gets in the way of work; it is inefficient. A sentence from another observation well summarizes much of what we saw and experienced: "Deadpan characteristics whatever is being said, whether praise or warning."

The suppression of the emotional between teachers and students is an important component of the program's commitment to obedience and orderliness. The quality and quantity of interaction is defined primarily by the nature of the task to be performed and only secondarily, if at all, by the personalities of those who are interacting. This helps keep things neat and orderly between teachers and students. They both know what is considered relevant and what is irrelevant; their interchanges are ideally as free of idiosyncratic personal qualities as possible, including humor. That which is not seemingly functional to the interaction's purposes is generally avoided. Hence interactions at Flowing Brook tend to be instrumental, and other potentially educative benefits of teacher-student interchanges are, by and large, lost. Occasionally students, as illustrated by Jacob, and to a degree teachers, steal brief moments for themselves. But these are *stolen* moments.

For the student such interactions, despite IGE talk about providing a "personalized" education, imply that worth comes primarily through accomplishing assigned tasks and demonstrating desired behaviors. Recognition and status can be earned by fitting in, for becoming a good student means being a reliable consumer of curriculum.

When the buzzer sounded indicating school was over, a change took place in Flowing Brook. As most of the children left school, a few stayed to interact with teachers. A good percentage of the teachers were engaged with students who wished to talk with them after school. At this time voices were transformed; they regained their energy. During the school day, it was generally not possible to make out distinct voices unless the talking was done close by. After school, however, voices became personal and more expressive. They were louder; laughter arose, and friendly teasing went on between students and teachers.

Anger is the one emotion that potentially could disrupt Flowing Brook's pleasantness. Anger often creeps up on us and appears without warning; other times it simmers, biding its time as frustrations pile on top of one another, only to explode at an inopportune moment: "If you don't knock that off, I'm going to knock your head off!" This was the one singular, uncharacteristic expression of strong teacher emotion voiced. Incidents of anger were usually short and created only a slight ripple in the otherwise smooth progress of the school day. It was as though anger, like losing pencils, was expected and prepared for so that it had minimal impact. The general type of angry confrontation present in Flowing Brook is indicated by observation:

> A teacher got really angry at a kid. She did not say anything to the child but picked her up by the shoulders and hustled her to the back of the class area, then thrust her brusquely down to the floor. Teacher was clearly miffed—livid really. The child said nothing, the teacher said nothing, and the rest of the class did not seem to notice anything. Routine continued; there was no disruption. Teacher immediately returned to her desk activities. Incident lasted about fifteen seconds.

Anger was present and then gone, short and quick. The routine of the day was unaffected. In this incident there was no verbal communication, no effort to try to understand one another better, no opportunity for the student to talk and, perhaps, no perceived need.

One other emotion, educationally perhaps the most significant, remains to be discussed. It is excitement. Normally we think of excitement being generated by learning that has somehow captured a student's imagination. In Flowing Brook we observed little excitement of any kind outside of recess. In fact excitement was taken to be undesirable, as indicated by the following observation. Two third/fourth–grade students had finished their work and with anticipation selected to fill their free time with a game of Battleship. They enthusiastically set up the game on the perimeter of the class and began to play. "They got a little (very little) noisy and without warning the teacher told them to put it away. They had gotten too excited." They put the game away without protest but very slowly while they continued to talk softly. Apparently they had gotten a bit too carried away with the game and with each other's company. For a moment they forgot where they were. They were quickly reminded; perhaps in the future they will be less likely to forget. It is difficult to imagine children playing games they care to play without getting a little noisy, but this seems to be what is expected in Flowing Brook. It is little wonder expressions of excitement associated with learning were so rarely observed.

It is not the case that there was no laughter, anger, or excitement in Flowing Brook. We did, however, see surprisingly little of it. The message of IGE is clear with respect to the value of emotion: That which does not foster program purposes is to be avoided and, where necessary, repressed.

Laughter or anger or excitement experienced by a class moves it in directions that cannot be easily predicted and likely will shorten lesson time. Such expressions may offer rare opportunities for learning, but that requires a level of teacher artistry and understanding incongruent with system-dictated role expectations.

To summarize, a system that restricts the range of acceptable emotional expression enables some things while limiting others. What is enabled is an increase in time spent learning specific skills and content, on order and quiet that will facilitate such learning, and perhaps most important, strengthening the legitimacy of a strict control of the behavior appropriate to a workplace. When one spends time in Flowing Brook as an observer, it becomes evident that children are learning to be effective in doing work that has little personal meaning but pays off in external rewards, the kind of work done in bureaucracies. What is limited is the opportunity to develop understanding and expression of a wide range of emotion. This is especially important in light of our concern for the development of critical-mindedness. Where emotion is blunted, the potential for sensing problems or, at the extreme, being outraged, is limited or perhaps lost. The capacity must be cherished. Without it intellectual attainment lacks heart and commitment. We turn now to consider how IGE restricts the role of intellect in the education of the young.

We shall discuss two aspects of the restriction of the intellect in Flowing Brook. The first has to do with what is most worth knowing while the second has to do with the nature of intellectual attainment itself. There are other related aspects that could be discussed here, such as the way knowledge is fragmented and the role testing plays in establishing what is to be learned, but these were treated in the preceding chapter.

We can ascertain what is viewed as worth knowing in Flowing Brook, the object of the intellectual life, by considering the nature of dialogue or intellectual interaction there. We focus on dialogue because it is profoundly important to becoming critically minded. Dialogue, as talk between mutually respectful inquirers, was seldom observed at Flowing Brook. Instead the so-called intellectual interactions that take place are usually structured recitations where teachers ask specific questions and students fill in the blanks. A typical discussion is described in this excerpt from our observations of a sixth-grade class:

> [Teacher talking] "How many watch 'Mr. Merlin'?" [Hands go up]. "How many like it?" [Most]. "How many don't like it?" [None]. He was using TV to get at some kind of literature concept—I missed this

part. He has the kids read from their magazines. When they finish he goes through the questions in the manual—a, b, c, d. The kids raise their hands on what they think is the right answer. He then tells them the truth, and they move on. There is no discussion of alternatives or of why one answer is preferred over another. The kids don't seem to expect such a discussion. Most of the questions get split responses— some of them get a near even split seeming to indicate the necessity of exploring differences. 10:30 — Stirring. Recess is near. Time considerations completely dominate the curriculum — obviously there was no discussion—there wasn't time.

The purpose of this discussion was not to share ideas or feelings nor was it to raise serious questions or to think. The students were to look for specific facts from a short piece of printed material and to prove having found the right fact by telling it to the class. Amassing such facts was the purpose of the lesson. The learning activity was the same kind as in the printed materials the students work through: Read a section and answer a list of questions. This can easily be done without interactions with a teacher. Many students are so used to this kind of procedure and so certain of their ability to fill in the blanks correctly that they raise their hands well before the teacher has finished articulating the question. They can do this because they know they will not need any time to think about their answers nor will there be any surprising twists in questioning; most important, they will not be expected to give reasons for their answers.

We can contrast this constricted kind of interaction with what it might be as dialogue. Dialogue is an exchange between persons who respect each other's need to know and who anticipate that each brings something worthwhile to the interaction. In other words intentions or seriousness of purpose and the intrinsic value of trying to understand are mutually honored in dialogue. These qualities must be no less present with children than with adults. That children and adults are unequal does not preclude dialogue because in some senses it always takes place between unequals, between persons whose knowledge and grasp are different, thereby permitting reciprocal enlightenment. Our perception was that because of their role as direction givers and work supervisors, teachers looked on dialogue with children as undesirable and perhaps impossible. Hence interactions seemed to be perfunctory and obligatory rather than interesting and pleasure giving.

Another aspect of dialogue that sets it apart from the type of interactions we observed in Flowing Brook is its intellectual content and quality.

At Flowing Brook interaction begins with factual questions and with calls for opinions that need neither explanation nor defense, one opinion being just as good as any other. Factual questions, while important to dialogue, are not sufficient. Interaction must go further, to considering the reasons why of things. Although considering the whys of something often generates tension between people, when this tension is embedded in respect and in the desire for understanding, it is highly positive for education. Thus students become motivated to find better, more reasoned explanations but less concerned with finding only correct answers. The stress upon the merely factual serves to mask the interests embedded in public knowledge or in common sense whereas questing after the whys opens the possibility of uncovering these interests. This process of seeking beyond the given or the taken-for-granted expresses our communication and emancipation interests.

It may appear to the reader that we are arguing for the impossible, that children demonstrate sophistication in dialoguing. But we must ask, how are children going to learn to dialogue if they are rarely exposed to the process? Biological maturity does not necessarily bring with it intellectual or emotional maturity. Rather, as with the ability to dialogue, these come with time and experience. The foundations of mature dialogue can and ought to be established early. We can turn to our teacher who asked questions about "Mr. Merlin" for some leads in this direction. The observation hints at what might have been possible. The teacher might have asked, for example, why some students came up with divergent answers from their reading. Were student conclusions contrary to the officially correct ones nevertheless reasonable? Upon what grounds did the students base their conclusions? Were there problems within the reading itself? Recall, these are questions about presumably factual matters.

Students in Flowing Brook need do little thinking. They are encouraged to be passive learners, mere consumers of knowledge, which is all of more or less equal worth. This consumer message communicates very clearly to the young that knowing is simply the ability to accumulate facts that others generate. Surely implicit is the view that one's own experience and feelings ought not to be taken too seriously as sources for understanding. Students are seldom encouraged to think about their own lives or to entertain options. In contrast dialogue necessarily honors experience, for all knowledge is, as Michael Polanyi reminds us, "personal knowledge," knowledge grounded in the personal-culture experience, the biography, of the knower.[3] Knowledge that is not so grounded is unusable, mere verbalisms: words without commitment or understanding. Questions that require only the facts demand very little emotionally or intellectually of the young. Because the young come to believe that they have little if any stake in what they must learn, they fail to understand how and why knowledge is power. For them knowledge is a commodity valued for its quick and easy payoff.

Intellectual achievement is homogenized at Flowing Brook. The program operates with the presumption that there are few qualitative differences between the intellectual expressions of bright and slow students. Hence homogeneous grouping, which ostensibly fosters progress at an individual's own best rate, in fact is really focused on group achievement in respect to some minimally acceptable standard test scores. In this view, higher-achieving students are supposed to accomplish X amount and lower-achieving students Y amount. But the difference between X and Y is held to be merely one of degree, not of kind or quality. Therefore lower achievers need only spend more time on the material than higher achievers in order to master the essentials of the curriculum. The tenet or program faith is that the more practice students get with what they will be tested on, the more likely they are to do well, or at least passably well. Therefore slow learners improve their scores while internalizing a false impression of what intellectual mastery means: mastery of minimums.

High achievers, however, are served badly by this process in two senses. First, what counts as intellectual achievement is essentially the accumulation of large bodies of facts. Intellectual excellence of a non-measurable kind, such as sensing ambiguity in an argument or writing a compelling sentence, is not highly honored. Second, all students, bright and slow alike, do the same kind of work. All children presumably master the same concepts in essentially the same ways, though there may be some minor variation of route. This usually means bright children do extra work or receive enrichment lessons. But even for those who receive enrichment, the concepts are the same. The only difference is that some children get to "explore" these concepts more fully; that is, do more of the same work but not creative intellectual activity. Bright students are kept busy but learn that further intellectual effort means more of the same, not new and important understandings. In general, however, the depth of understanding achieved is roughly the same for all students: the minimum has become the maximum.

Thus far we have discussed the manner in which life in Flowing Brook restricts what we take as normal and desirable expressions of childhood.

The young learn to restrain their expressions of emotion and of intellect. In particular, they learn to channel their intellectual efforts by containing curiosity; they keep their noses in their books. While such behavior is generally taken as highly desirable, it does run counter to some other deeply held American values having to do with thinking and acting independently. We turn next to why this tension between educational values goes unacknowledged.

TECHNOLOGICAL LANGUAGE AND EDUCATION

Language affects what we see and what we think. We are in a sense victims of its power to define reality for us. Hence the language of technological curriculum programs such as IGE profoundly informs our descriptions of schooling activities like teaching and learning. By virtue of the predominance of these programs, educational processes are taken as equivalent to their technological descriptions. The understandings of teachers and administrators are thereby limited, and their educational efforts become tightly focused in specific directions. IGE language encourages some schooling practices, as we have shown, but it also discourages others. It discourages the likelihood that questions and tensions among teachers, parents, and students about educational values—about what is being done and what is believed should be done—will arise to become issues of educational importance, to become part of the curriculum. To put it another way, IGE descriptions enable teachers to focus on particular activities and outcomes while constraining their ability to respond to or even to recognize program effects that deviate from those discussed in the literature. Under the persuasiveness of a seemingly scientific research and development, words commonly used to describe human activities and qualities are rendered more limited in their meanings by giving them restricted, technical definitions.

The purpose of IGE, as the name says, is to produce individualized or personalized education. By design IGE programs are supposed to "facilitate each student's development in the cognitive, psychomotor, and affective domains of learning."[4] This surely suggests that an IGE program will be respectful of and responsive to the uniqueness of each student. Student development is to be fostered via an instructional program that "assumes active learning, continuous pupil progress, and personalized instruction . . . adapted to the rate of learning and other characteristics of the individual."[5] This requires, the IGE literature states, that "materials, activities, time, and teacher direction are purposefully varied to meet the needs of individual students."[6] Thus personalized instruction should transcend merely adapting materials and processes to the child's rate and style of learning; other desirable educational outcomes should be promoted. And indeed IGE claims that "through personal attention from a team of teachers, each student will be aided in developing a positive regard for self along with self-control, personal responsibility and social responsibility."[7]

It is difficult to disagree with a program that is personalized and one in which students are viewed as active learners working on tasks that are appropriate for meeting their particular needs. Because we generally do not have specific definitions in mind for these positive phrases—*meeting particular needs, personalized instruction, active learners*—we take them to be describing a curriculum that will help students grow. However, as we have shown in our accounts of schooling at Flowing Brook, there seems to be an incongruity between the IGE description of its purposes and programs and what takes place in an IGE school. But that incongruity is only apparent, for in IGE the meanings of many of the most essential words are narrowed to the extent that what appears to be on first reading a description of a richly human program is actually that of a carefully designed technical one.

The use of personalized instruction is indicative of the technical emphasis of the program. The focus here is not on what the uniqueness of each child suggests for elementary schooling but rather on "three critical matters dealing with units of instruction: . . . (1) whether the objectives incorporated in the unit are to be attained by all students, (2) whether the criteria that are specified for attainment of the objectives are the same for all students, and (3) whether the units of instruction are to be taken in a fixed sequence."[8] Clearly the central concern of IGE, as that of GEMS, is with objectives and the content that students are required to learn. While some variation is allowed, it is evident that the differences are small. The first "critical matter"—whether objectives are to be attained by all students—provides variety only within the range of content already selected. The second — whether specified criteria are the same for all students — is merely an issue of evaluation. The "critical matter" seems much the same, especially in practice, as asking whether all students must receive A's or, perhaps more to the point, whether all grades should mean the same. The final concern—whether the units must be taken in a fixed sequence—gives only a superficial sense of choice where no genuine alternatives are allowed. Surely if all units must be studied, then sequence of study changes little. Hence the use of *personalized* seems to mean little more than some instructional flexibility for the teacher and limited options for children. It is not a concern for individual needs and interests.

Since instruction is centered on objectives linked to specific skills and content, it is worth noting some of the characteristics of the content that is to be learned. For IGE, what is to be learned must be free from "cultural bias and factual errors" as well as free of "possible misinterpretations."[9] The technological bias of IGE is of course a cultural bias, awareness of which is precluded by technocratic-mindedness. It appears that subject matter, the creation of human beings, is to be washed clean of the taint of humanness—the interpretations and arguments that make up our attempt to understand. Evidently students are to learn efficiently a series of skills and ideas supporting a particular view of the world, and to make what can only be called indoctrination more palatable, it is touted as "personalized instruction."

If it is understood that in IGE usage the word *personalization* means instructional flexibility, then our account of life at Flowing Brook accords with IGE's self-description. Students at Flowing Brook all work on the same kinds of tasks, but they do use different materials and do accomplish different amounts in a given time. And since this is done in the name of personalized instruction, the program tends to constrain busy teachers from raising questions about or recognizing that their activity has little to do with the education of individual persons and much to do with training the masses.

The use of the concept *active learning* is an example of how meaning becomes distorted through program emphasis. For most of us, active learning suggests that the person takes part in deciding what to learn and that the study is therefore interesting and not merely required. We also generally associate active learning with an active mind, with questioning and striving to understand. This sense of learning is held to be quite the opposite of merely going through the motions while "feeling outside himself," to use Karl Marx's description of the capitalist worker. The problem in IGE is that while active learning is identified as important, the requirements that teaching be guided by predetermined objectives and that "means of assessing each student's attainment of each objective are necessary" divert attention from considering students' engagement to proving they have reached program objectives.[10] The proof is furnished by a method that will "measure accurately the performances implied by the objectives."[11] At Flowing Brook objectives are selected by others, and the obsession with accurate measurement translates into busy rather than active learners. This change from active learners to busy workers masks the important distinction between passive acceptance and active participation in deciding what and how to learn. Furthermore, as long as assigned tasks are completed, teachers are not likely to question whether students find their work meaningful. Thus possible areas of tension and therefore of development are lost.

As might be anticipated from a technological education program, the needs of students are determined for them by assessment instruments. "Each student must be assessed in order to plan an appropriate instructional program for the student as well as to ascertain attainment of the objectives of each unit of the instructional sequence."[12] *Need* cannot mean something students feel or can identify for themselves but must be determined for them by an objectified process. Again, for technological programs the word *need* indicates a person's lack of something — skills, attributes, attitudes — that a system requires for its functioning. While normal or common use of the word *need* suggests that educational attention might be paid to students' attempts to understand their circumstances, the actual program emphasis is a conservative, status-quo–preserving interpretation of society's need for people with particular skills and attitudes. The way that the term *need* is used in the IGE literature indicates that there should be no conflict between what people want for themselves and what the status quo requires of them. This is an outlook that mystifies rather than clarifies, for it suppresses the tensions that normally exist and should exist between personal desires and the requirements of society by defining the needs of the individual as those of the system. This shift of meaning is especially important because if children and their teachers can be convinced that their personal needs are legitimately defined by society, then little if any possibility remains for personal autonomy. When individuality is submerged within the group, the few get to decide what is best for the many. Thus that which is deemed good for meeting social needs is held as good, right, and appropriate for meeting individual needs. Those who resist these decisions are considered aberrant. Normal students (and good citizens) work contentedly at meeting their socially defined personal needs.

A careful look at the literature of the two programs discussed this far, GEMS and IGE, reveals that they use language in similar ways. They each combine technical jargon: *topic inventory, management system, guides to informal individual skill observations,* with educational psychology terms such as *construct validity,* and *criterion-referenced measurement* and words having a humanistic appeal such as the three discussed above, *personalized instruction, active learning,* and *individual needs.* The humanistic words are used to obscure the actual meaning—and perhaps the intent—of the programs. In the descriptive literature of the programs, in the talk of teachers, and in the classrooms of GEMS and IGE, it is the use of technology to control behavior that is the overpowering though not explicitly stated curriculum. In these programs the language of science and the language of humanism are skillfully manipulated to enhance and maintain technocratic-mindedness. In this process words get stringently narrowed in meaning, providing only technical descriptions for human activities.

The result is that the language of the technological curriculum serves to legitimate control. It does so not by demonstrating its need but covertly, by using words normally connoting freedom and choice in such constrained, unusual ways that they end up meaning system control. Of course this is not a carefully planned plot by educational researchers to subjugate students, but it happens because, as we discussed in chapter 1, educational research is grounded in the positivistic outlook that assumes creating better education means studying human beings with the same methods used to study the physical world. The following discussion of the research and development efforts of IGE shows how a technical interest in control is generalized to all human interests.

IGE was developed and continues to be developed through what is called programmatic research:

> Programmatic research in education is mission oriented. It is directed toward identifying a significant problem area and conducting research to gain more information about the problem area. The results of this research then contribute to the development of procedures, processes, materials, and other products which will reduce or eliminate certain identified problems. [13]

Research is oriented to problems such as how to improve reading comprehension. The first step is to think of some promising techniques and by a procedure of trying and refining, to create a method of instruction that is likely to be more effective than those in use. To determine whether the new is better than the old, educators compare student test scores, using sophisticated statistical procedures. If the statistical treatment shows that groups taught with the new method better comprehend what they read than groups taught with other methods, then it is possible to form a generalization that goes something like this: Students taught using procedure X score higher on measure Y than students taught by a different procedure. Such generalizations, when produced through careful research, hold the same status as generalizations about the physical world: They are accepted as hard, true facts. How can one argue against statistical proof?

Our purpose here is not to refute the assumptions about human beings that underly such research, though we believe this can be done, but rather to point out that the generalizations coming from this research become teaching procedures that must be carefully followed in order to get specific, valued outcomes. One explanation for the obsession with efficiency and control that we observed at Flowing Brook is that teachers feel they must follow the program as written because it has been found better, proven by unquestionable, scientific methods. Schooling practices thus are focused on using the identified means to reach the predetermined outcomes that support the findings from research. And this is what education means within IGE.

Acceptance of IGE and its attendant mindedness enables educators to produce certain effects such as higher achievement test scores but limits their ability to see that other, more significant results also occur. In Flowing Brook students learn by doing orderly work in carefully sequenced materials. At the same time, they learn to conform and not to question. They learn to compartmentalize their life activities, and in general they learn to become technocratically rather than critically minded. When we observe what students and teachers do, when we examine the whole gamut of schooling practices instead of just testing and scores, the desirability of IGE becomes problematic. For as our description of Flowing Brook shows, certain actions and attitudes are indeed acquired by young people. But when the acquisition of these actions and attitudes is ensured, different, more human ones are inhibited. Philosophic-mindedness may be lost for never having had a chance to be cultivated.

Chapter 4

Art and the
Technocratic
Imperative

In the preceding chapters, we examined how technocratic-mindedness informs teachers' thinking about education and affects the quality of school life for teachers and students. In this chapter we explore yet another aspect of the domination of technocratic-mindedness over the curriculum. Specifically we focus on how technocratic values determine the way marginal content areas and educational experiences must establish their legitimacy within the curriculum.

Curriculum in a general sense is an expression of selected values a culture desires to transmit to the young. Obviously not all that is valued can or need be transmitted through schooling: Schools, after all, are not churches or army brigades. Decisions about what should be taught in school are at once both ideological and technical. They are ideological in the sense that schools — understood as cultural delivery systems — will transmit only some values and not others. They will emphasize, for example, citizenship as voting but not as the practice of civil disobedience. Similarly, as we have argued, the form or pattern that curriculum making takes, its technical aspects, also puts limits on what can be delivered or transmitted. The form the curriculum takes is an illustration of the mindedness of the culture. The technological form of curriculum (e.g., GEMS, IGE) determines what students are taught partly because it is easier to teach some aspects of a subject using this form than others. Those aspects of curriculum unamenable to the form may be simply excluded or become supplementary. The arts are especially difficult to adapt to a technological curriculum form. Those interested in the arts argue that they are a distinct and uniquely human endeavor that should be appreciated and understood by all members of society and therefore need to be taught in the schools. But in most public schools, particularly elementary schools, little teaching of the arts takes place. One reason seems to be that except for significantly talented students, the arts are not germane to the type of vocational training we found, for example, at Flowing Brook. Another reason might be that the arts are recognized as an implied danger to the status quo, for they communicate images and provide understandings that question what we unthinkingly accept as natural, necessary, and right. They hold the potential to suggest that things might be looked at differently, that life might be lived otherwise.

If we are correct that the pervasive mindedness of our time is the technocratic, then this should show up in the treatment of art by the public schools. Surely some support for our view is the fact that there is so little teaching of the arts. But a more telling confirmation of our thesis is what happens to the arts when well-meaning art educators try to induce schools to teach them by organizing instruction according to the technological curriculum form. For the art educator, the adoption of the technological form involves a sharp trade-off between what is enabled by this particular way of organizing subject matter for teaching and what is limited by it. This trade-off is seldom recognized clearly although it may be hazily sensed or dimly understood. As we argued in chapter 1, this lack of recognition is a partial consequence of technocratic-mindedness, which limits the ability to conceive of any state of affairs other than the given and approved. (An alternative may be thought desirable but not possible, for reason is bound by instrumental constraints.) The subject matter that cannot fit into this form is tangential. Please note that it is not necessarily undesirable; it is simply unessential. Such a point of view, of course, supports the conviction of the technological experts that their curriculum decisions are firmly scientific and objective and totally value neutral.

For marginal content areas or ones that have not established themselves, this outlook presents unique problems. For in order to establish or to preserve their place, such areas ought to be organized according to the dominant pattern. But such organization may also cause significant changes in the character, purposes, and meaningfulness of that content. This is the trade-off for the art educator faced with adopting the technological curriculum form. Something indeed is gained — a place in the curriculum—but something is also lost—perhaps that which makes art a worthwhile, unique human activity.

In this chapter we will explore in detail what happens to the visual arts when they are organized by the technological curriculum form. We begin our analysis by considering problems of legitimacy. We are using the term *legitimacy* to mean the grounds upon which proponents establish the worth of a content area or educational experience and the form of the argument they present. (*Content area* means the segment of our cultural tradition that we wish to transmit to the young through schooling.) The goal of those seeking to establish legitimacy is to convince others of the merit of their points of view in hopes of getting time and money allotted to their content area—reading, driver training, aerobics, computers, or whatever.

LEGITIMACY

Questions of legitimacy are always important in curriculum decisions, for every epoch and every interest group has its view of what knowledge is of most worth, of what children should be learning. During this century such questions have become urgent because a proliferation of supposedly necessary subject matter has meant keen competition for the limited time of students. Furthermore, in hard economic times cuts in school programs are inevitable and most likely to fall on those content areas that have inadequately established or maintained their legitimacy.

Historically the issue of legitimacy is well illustrated by the case of Greek and Latin in the public school curriculum. Study of these languages had long been a main course in the intellectual diet of students. Around the turn of the century, faculty psychology, which had justified the value of these subjects, was discredited. Faculty psychology had provided the rationale for the view that because Greek and Latin were difficult subjects, they were essential to molding disciplined minds, training reasoning powers, and developing memory. As long as these subjects were assumed to be the most effective means for producing intellectual discipline, their position within the curriculum was secure. When faculty psychology came to be widely questioned, their educational worth had to be established on other grounds. Their champions, the teachers and professors of classical languages, failed to do so, and first Greek and then Latin gradually fell into disfavor. Greek has virtually disappeared from the curriculum while Latin may still be found here and there in high schools priding themselves as strongly academic. With their demise classical languages were replaced by a number of subjects whose legitimacy rested on their usefulness to a rapidly industrializing nation.

To explore how technocratic-mindedness defines the terms upon which legitimacy is established and thereby limits the possibilities of curriculum change, we chose to focus on the art curriculum. The arts have long been a part of the curriculum, but their position has generally been tenuous. In the elementary school, for example, art activities — not the study of art — rarely take up more than half an hour to one hour per week. Further, when such activities are more extensive, it is often because they are used to fill up the free time of students who finish their assignments ahead of others or as rewards for good behavior. Many worksheets, for instance, incorporate so-called art activities such as coloring as time fillers. Typically students who finish their worksheets early in math find the outline of a clown or an elephant to be colored in at the bottom of the page.

School critics have traditionally valued the arts as the content area in which young people can be relatively free to express themselves. For the young, doing art is an expression of their need to communicate. They draw without prompting and enjoy sharing the activities with others. Ironically the marginal position of the arts in the curriculum has allowed their use for enhancing the values of creative expression. Because the doing of art has been looked on as its own reward, good simply in the doing, there has not in general been an urgent call to systematize art instruction. But whether the arts even could be organized systematically for instructing the young has been something of a persistent curriculum question. On the negative side, because of the lack and seeming impossibility of systematization and due to children's spontaneous engagement with art activities, many educators have regarded the area as rather unimportant, as essentially irrelevant to the school's contribution to children's development. In such cases little if any art gets into the curriculum.

The problem then for those interested in the arts is to make certain that teachers who emphasize them will continue to do so while those who do not become more involved. Yet how is this to be accomplished when even the tenuous position of the arts in the curriculum is threatened by our escalated concern for the so-called basic skill areas? Unfortunately the arts must compete with the basic skills. But what happens to their potential for eliciting free expression and creativity from the young when their legitimacy must be established in terms appropriate only for the inculcation of skills? Phrased differently, what happens to the arts when they are controlled by the technocratically minded?

AIE: A PROGRAM FOR SYSTEMATIC ART TEACHING

We selected for study a visual arts program entitled Art Is Elementary (AIE).[1] We focused our attention primarily on the published curriculum guide, though to better understand how it was conceived and used we went out into the field. Interviews were conducted with one of the developers, a district art specialist who runs a teacher in-service program and is piloting the tests, and a number of teachers representing two districts. In addition we observed classes and attended an in-service session.

AIE is a response to questions about the legitimacy of art in the curriculum and to the related problem of criticism of elementary school art teaching. Before considering AIE in detail, we will make a general comment about a perplexing problem the developers faced. On the one hand, they were interested in preserving and extending the expressive potential of art. On the other hand, they wanted to build a program that would meet the current conditions for establishing legitimacy. In important respects these two goals are contradictory, and the attempt to fit them together underlies the confusion in the program.

AIE was a result of a statewide curriculum reform effort established by the Utah state superintendent of public instruction. Individual schools throughout the state were designated as centers for developing curriculum in specific content areas. State, district, and school personnel worked together in these centers to design prototype programs that eventually were tested and refined in other schools throughout the state. One elementary school was responsible for developing the visual arts program. The state art specialist, district art supervisor, and others came together with the teachers to build a program where none existed before.

Through their deliberations the committee members discovered that an art program was, as one member related, "impossible to organize . . . with the [traditional] product approach." Typically elementary school art teaching focuses on the making of products of various kinds. For example, as we reported, in our visits to Flowing Brook during the Christmas season, we observed students making identical construction-paper Santas. In two fourth-grade classes during this season, the students fashioned clay pots as gifts for their mothers. Both of these activities are examples of the product approach to art teaching.

This approach to art in the elementary schools does not lend itself to the development of a program unless *program* is understood as merely a list of art activities teachers should have their students do during the school year. This was not however the meaning held by those charged with developing the art curriculum. In curriculum circles programs are understood to include statements of purpose, a sequence of means—activities, materials, and so on—to accomplish these purposes, and provision for evaluation. The product approach to art is hardly systematic, does not lend itself to evaluation; and has as its purpose *doing*, and doing one thing is usually perceived as just as good as doing anything else. The doing, the making, is its own end; it is not presumed to add up to any particular understanding or skill.

While the committee struggled with the problem of making a program, of creating a systematic approach to the organization, teaching, and evaluating of art, some of its members were also involved in another indirectly related state curriculum effort on individualizing instruction. This project sought to identify the fundamental concepts in various content areas and to write sequenced lists of performance objectives that would, when taken together, presumably add up to concept understanding or mastery. From these efforts the idea gradually emerged within the committee that art too could be approached conceptually. This insight revealed the possibility of producing the desired program in the arts.

Once the idea was grasped that art education could be approached conceptually, then, as one of its developers recalled in a recorded interview, "Everything else kind of fell into place." This committee's fundamental principle was that art could be taught and learned like any other subject that seemed to involve mastering certain skills (called *concepts* in AIE). For the student therefore, learning to draw, paint, weave—make art — was viewed as precisely equivalent to learning to read or to ride a bicycle. Supposedly there is a proper sequence of small necessary steps to be taken in learning to ride a bicycle that if strictly followed will result in virtually anyone mastering the skill or so-called concept of bike riding. And as it is with reading, arithmetic, and bike riding, the skills and concepts to be learned in art are also behaviorally defined and thus amenable to measurement and evaluation.

From the committee's initial insight, it took nine years to develop Art

Is Elementary. It took so long partly because the developers wanted to involve teachers in every stage of the construction process—identifying concepts, creating a lesson format, and so on. College and high school art teachers also contributed significantly to the project because the committee aimed at producing a completely articulated program. The elementary school would teach "basic concepts," and advanced work would follow in the junior and senior high schools.

Eventually 206 concepts were identified that "could be applied in any mode or fashion with any type of media." Included in this list are such concepts as texture, harmony, balance, light, shadow, and perspective. With the help of teachers, lessons were developed that include performance objectives, suggestions of activities and materials, and evaluation procedures. Teachers are urged to plug their own activities into the lessons where appropriate. The lessons are organized in what AIE claims is a "logical, developmental order" that supposedly moves from simple to complex skills and concepts.[2] And following this order is declared to be essential for teaching success. The program, the developers state, "is designed to teach students how to increase their skills in both understanding and doing. This means that the teacher must present the concepts in sequence and at a time or level appropriate for the learner. . . . learning will not take place if the instruction is out of sequence or if the instruction is given before the child is mentally or physically ready for the experience."[3]

No doubt children will find learning difficult or impossible if they are not developmentally ready; this is a simple truism. But developmental readiness is not the same as a necessary sequence of learning activities. It must be shown by those making this claim that the sequence is, for instance, precisely coordinated with developmental facts or that there are other compelling reasons—it exemplifies behavior modification theory, say—for asserting that "learning will not take place if the instruction is out of sequence." AIE does not provide any such demonstration or set of compelling reasons. Rather it merely conflates two issues, a truism—readiness—with a bold declaration—necessary sequence—anticipating perhaps that the developmental fact will provide a sort of support by association for the unsubstantiated claim.

According to AIE, when all the concepts are "linked together," they "will provide the significant base of knowledge each individual needs in art education."[4] Of course, what each individual needs in art education is determined by the program and the constraints it labors under. The concepts are categorized as "skill" and "awareness" concepts although the difference between them is never clarified, and they both deal with "two and three dimensional ideas," for example, drawing and modeling. The concepts are declared to be geared to "eight different levels of under-standing and competency—or student 'readiness'—and are" supposedly in a "sequence for systematic growth and progression."[5] Again, just what "systematic growth and progression" is supposed to mean is unexplained.

Students are assessed for placement within one of the eight develop-mental levels (preschool to seventh grade) represented in the program. (Note that *developmental levels* simply means grades in school.) This assessment is made by comparing a student's drawings of "subject matter common to his experience" to the "diagnostic charts" composed of illustra-tions of children's artwork organized to indicate levels of understanding and competence as defined by the program.[6] We have already seen that this is arbitrary and ambiguous. In this way teachers may either group their students — two to five groups is suggested — or teach whole classes beginning at the "low average" level. Regardless of placement the sequence is essentially the same for all students.

In their desire to produce a program for teaching art, the committee members started with a notion of correct curriculum form that is used in the skill areas. They did not move from a particular understanding of art or esthetics to the development of a program; rather they moved from a particular pattern of curriculum development to the content area. What is noteworthy about this move from program pattern to content area is how the subject matter, the visual arts, is changed in the process and how the purposes for teaching art come to be heavily colored by purposes accepted as legitimate in the skill areas, much as traditionally liberal subjects such as English and mathematics, have become heavily colored by purposes appropriate to career and vocational education.

The influence of this procedure on the content of the visual arts shows up in some surprising ways. In order to organize the arts conceptually, the developers defined the term *concept* in a peculiar manner. Concepts are ideas, theoretical constructs (the atom), universal or abstract notions (democracy, a triangle, happiness) — in essence, something conceived mentally rather than given through experience, like the hand on the hot stove. In a less formal sense, we might use the word *concept* to mean an overarching idea by which we order our perceptions. Thus we might speak of the concept of ecology or of having an ecological outlook to indicate our general standpoint on land use and development, wilderness, conservation, animal life, and so on. What then do the developers of AIE mean when they state that their program is organized around "awareness" and "skill" concepts? What is an "awareness concept" or a "skill concept," and how do they differ?

Awareness concepts appear to include two elements: true concepts such as "order" and, strangely, generalizations that call attention to the relations between concepts. (Generalizations differ from concepts by making statements about our experiences, our observations, or our comparisons of individual facts and appearances.) Examples of such generalizations are "People and objects vary in size" (activity 60) and "People and objects appear smaller as they get further away" (activity 76). Perhaps it is thought that tagging the phrase *awareness concept* onto such unremarkable, commonplace, and obvious experiences raises these statements from triviality to importance. Awareness concepts are apparently distinguished from skill concepts by instructional intent rather than by differences in the nature of the content to be covered. That is, most awareness concepts seemed to be concerned with getting the student to develop a disposition to recognize, for example, that "dark values seem optically 'heavier' than light values" (activity 96). Where the instructional intention is to facilitate the development of a particular skill as, for instance, "The student uses a variety of washes in painting with water base media" (activity 128) or "The student can create a variety of forms by laminating thin sheets of various materials" (activity 190), then apparently we have a skill concept.

If this is meant essentially as a pedagogical distinction, it has dubious value, for closer scrutiny suggests that awareness concepts are often to be understood as skill concepts. For instance, the distinction between skill in "seeing" that a particular representation illustrates the application of a concept is not clearly differentiated from skill in "doing," in actually applying the concept. This failure is illustrated by such concepts as "Now the child should be aware of the following photography precepts: loading films into a camera, processing negatives, enlargements and how to use a viewfinder" (activity 52). Is this a skill or an awareness concept? And does it make any difference which it is? In short, in order to fit the content of the visual arts into a concept format, the word *concept* has become hopelessly confused, resulting in ambiguity about the content and purposes of visual art teaching and learning.

Likely this confusion was recognized by those who developed the program, but why would they persist in it? It appears that they did so in part for strategic reasons. To build a systematic program in the arts and therefore to build a case for legitimacy, it was considered necessary to use the language of concepts. It is important to note that although the meaning of *concept* was confused, virtually no harm was done to the adopted pattern of curriculum development. The confusion only somewhat increased the difficulty of defining the concepts in operational terms that could be easily tested. The attempted resolution of this difficulty provides an interesting example of the reductionism that technocratic-mindedness perpetrates in curriculum development.

Almost every concept stated in the program is really a generalization. A signficant proportion of these, including many of those categorized as awareness concepts, imply rules to be followed in the production of works of art. They say, essentially, Do X and effect Y will be achieved. The following are typical examples: "Overlapping objects can be used to create an illusion of depth" (activity 65) and "Distant objects appear as a mass or as combinations of forms as their detail seems to diminish" (activity 89). The rule implicit in the first example is that if an illusion of depth is desired — or assigned — then overlapping is necessary. The rule implicit in the second example is that if an effect of distance is desired — or required — then the subject matter should be blurred or lack detail.

These rules have a status equivalent to the rules in mathematics or language. They are a grammar for art, guides to acceptable usage or to correct procedures for producing art. Importantly, the identification of such generalizations as awareness concepts, removes much of the normal distinction between awareness and skill. That is to say, awareness — seeing, observing — comes to be defined as a skill — doing, making. The result is that the emphasis that is widely held as central in art education — to develop esthetic awareness — is significantly diminished. Understanding or awareness in some measure is reduced to doing. And while skills of doing are surely involved in understanding and appreciating art, nevertheless understanding and appreciating cannot be reduced to skills of doing. Relatively few of us can be skillful in the doing of art, but all of us can become more sensitive in our appreciation of it because appreciation is a facet of our total understanding, the growth of which is the proper aim of emancipatory education. But, crucially, skills lend themselves to quantified evaluations more readily than do understandings.

This reductive process continues in recent partial revisions of Art Is Elementary. Some concepts have been removed and others rewritten in attempts to clear up confusions, and currently only "essential understanding(s)" remain. Moreover student objectives have been reworked to better serve evaluation. Unfortunately the interest in greater precision has led to an even sharper focus on doing. Evaluation, for example, is primarily concerned with application: The student "draws," "names," "paints," "produces," "uses," "rearranges," "makes," "mixes," "rolls," and "applies." The student apparently does not express, explore, reveal, or create.

The lesson format also demonstrates reduction to a narrow doing. The opportunities to draw (recall, these are young children ranging from preschool age to approximately age twelve) are tightly bound by the assignments: to produce, for instance, "a picture in which vertical objects such as trees and chimneys are straight up and down" (lesson 59, revision). In short, students of whatever age or ability are expected to fit their expressive interest into a particular form. Hence the purpose of art education is to demonstrate the acquisition of a skill, called a concept, that can be easily evaluated.

INSTITUTIONALIZING AIE

The impact of the pattern of curriculum development on the purposes of art education is profound. Art of course is widely understood as valuable as its own end, needing no further justification for its being. The arts express our unique human and humanizing ability to transcend constraints; to imagine things otherwise as they might be or should be, not just as they are; to enliven, deepen, enrich, and to beautify the everyday. For most young people, artwork is fun and interesting for its own sake—before, at least, they learn to judge their work negatively, at which point an emphasis on craft or skill development seems appropriate. All these purposes, acknowledged by art specialists and craftsmen alike as legitimate, cannot be adequately treated or, more likely, even recognized by the adopted curriculum pattern.

But the case made for inclusion of art in the elementary school curriculum is not argued on the grounds that art has its own virtue. It is based instead on a general transference argument. An interviewee urged that art is perhaps the best way to "develop analysis or problem-solving skill." Further the AIE program guide states that "visual thinking skills and evaluative processes will lead students to responsible value judgments that will carry over to all areas of life."[7] Art education is thus supposed to be an omnibus means for developing mental and moral discipline. Children will become both better citizens and better problem solvers as a result of the AIE curriculum. Not too long ago, Latin and Greek were expected to accomplish those ends too. The idea evidently dies hard. (Interestingly a really sound education in art could indeed enhance analytical skills and moral grasp, but in that way lies radical analysis, confrontation with the status quo, and citizenship that acts for equality, rights, and democracy.) The major point of justification and the major purposes of art education for the AIE developers therefore are external to the subject matter. Whatever good may come from art education, we are entreated, will be found outside art itself.

Peculiarly missing here is the understanding that there is something distinctively worthwhile about teaching, learning, and engaging in art. Yet it is likely that those who developed the program hold to this view. If there is little that is distinctive, one must ask, why should art be in the curriculum at all? There are certainly more direct and influential ways of developing good citizens and problem solvers than through art education. This outlook is no improvement over the view that art is worthwhile because it breaks up the monotony of the day and is an important reward to students who get their work done.

Why would the developers choose to build their case for the arts on such weak grounds? The approach they chose for the development of Art Is Elementary and their willingness to adjust content to the curriculum pattern suggest that they saw no other way of producing something that would be widely recognized as a program. They grasped the fact that there is currently only one acceptable way to produce curriculum, to make what can be called a program. Thus the apparent relief of committee members when they discovered that art could be packaged in this way and their apparent failure to comprehend their distorted use of the term *concept*. We take this as an important indication of how technocratic-mindedness dominates even among art educators. But this does not directly address why it is that curriculum developers who recognize some of the limitations of this pattern choose to maintain it nevertheless.

Some insight into this problem comes from considering the impact of *Educational Programs That Work*, a publication of the Department of Education, National Diffusion Network Division, on the thinking of some of those involved in producing Art Is Elementary.[8] A word of caution is in order here. We do not wish to make too much of this influence because in some respects it is minor; however, it is also a clear illustration of the institutionalization of the dominant curriculum pattern and therefore of technocratic-mindedness. Institutionalization allows only certain methods and procedures and thereby helps block the creation of alternatives.

One of AIE's developers, a man sensitive to some of the weaknesses of the curriculum pattern adopted, told us that he and others involved in the program desired to get their work broadly disseminated. Such a goal is of course shared by most curriculum workers, for whom having a program operating in one school or district is not sufficient. The developers of AIE believe it promises great improvements in art teaching and thus deserves to become widely known and adopted. One way of furthering this goal— though not of accomplishing it — is to get the program accepted for publication in *Educational Programs That Work*.

To be accepted there, a program must meet rigorous standards established by the Joint Dissemination Review Panel. The panel uses eight "review criteria" in making its judgments: (1) evidence of impact, (2) interpretability of measures (which includes assessment of the type of instruments used and their reliability and validity), (3) credibility of the evidence, (4) evidence of statistical reliability of effects, (5) evidence that the effects are educationally meaningful, (6) evidence that the effects are attributable to the intervention, (7) evidence of generalizability, and (8) cost effectiveness.[9] Application of these standards results in the rejection of approximately half of the programs that apply for recognition. The vast majority of the cases made for program effectiveness are, of course, made statistically — recall, an important assumption of technocratic-mindedness is that the methods of the positive or natural sciences are more likely to produce reliable knowledge. Thus either standardized tests are used or tests are developed to make comparisons between control and treatment groups; a pretest-posttest format provides data, and a statistical significance of differences is established. Other approaches to proving program effectiveness are in principle possible but rarely developed because of cost and the difficulty of building a convincing case upon generally unacceptable grounds or through unusual procedures. Those who choose this route have to make two arguments; one for the design utilized and the other for the program itself. One researcher currently in the process of presenting a program for inclusion nicely sums up the reasons for sticking with the dominant pattern of establishing proof, even when he considers others more desirable. "It is," he said, "easier."

To these art educators, it is especially important to get into *Educational Programs That Work* because districts rarely embrace programs in the arts. This probably reflects a general attitude that art either cannot be programmed or does not merit the cost of building or adopting a program. Against the former attitude, inclusion demonstrates that art education can be systematic and efficiently taught, learned, and evaluated. Against the latter attitude, it suggests that art education can be an important means for achieving a variety of highly desired outcomes (e.g., respect for authority and sound work habits). Moreover, inclusion in *Educational Programs That Work* means eligibility for federal dissemination funds, an important benefit in hard times.[10]

Cost effectiveness is one of the eight review criteria of the Joint Dissemination Review Panel and therefore relevant to recognition by *Educational Programs That Work*. To speak of art education in efficiency terms such as cost effectiveness seems incongruous and basically wrong-headed. Nevertheless it is necessary for the curriculum developers to use such categories because programs establish their worth by demonstrating that they will foster the dominant technocratic values of our society. From the prospect of these values, the child is looked upon as a kind of product that should contain as many approved features as the school can build in under the limitation of time and expense. As a marginal content area, art receives at best only small amounts of school-day time; hence speed and efficiency are especially important. Indeed a strong case is made by the developers of AIE that the program is good because it systematically organizes the visual arts so that they can be taught quickly and efficiently. But surely one must ask what relationship speed and efficiency have to acquiring esthetic understanding? What is the real concern here: to have teachers cover as many lessons as possible or to have students understand and appreciate the visual arts?

The institutionalization of Art Is Elementary also seems to require descriptions in psychological categories and terms instead of the seemingly more appropriate ones of philosophical, esthetic, or artistic talk. The problems this creates are similar to the linguistic difficulties we discussed with GEMS and IGE — imprecision, ambiguity, mystification, and confusion. The language of measurement psychology is the language of justification in curriculum, a lingo of statistical differences. Even those who do not understand psychological theories are compelled to use this language which, as we have previously shown, is primarily one of prediction and control, hardly suitable to understanding expressions of our emancipation and communication interests.

Although within the program the terminologies of behaviorism, developmentalism, concept formation, and Gestalt psychology are indiscriminately intermixed, sometimes in the same sentence and without any sensitivity to how differences in theory affect differences in practice, the prevailing influence is an educational version of behavioral psychology. For example, lessons are presented as narrowly additive. They are supposed to show a logical movement from simple to complex in such a way that the parts, when learned in the proper order, are equivalent to the whole. The belief is apparent in the claim that learning will not occur "if the instruction is out of sequence."[11] This view of learning allows little place for intuition or insight or the student's personal integration of new learnings into what she already knows. Rather it is presumed that the student should and will integrate what is to be learned in the same way that the content is presented, seriatim in small, discrete steps.

The indiscriminate mixing of theories and languages is common in curriculum development, where eclecticism is considered a virtue. Unfortunately one result of eclecticism is that meaning is often obscured and substance mystified by high-sounding phrases: "The concepts are geared to eight different levers of understanding and competency — or student 'readiness' — and are in a sequence for systematic growth and progression." This sounds impressive, suggesting that AIE provides teachers with a series of lessons arranged in and grounded on a developmentally rigorous order. However in the actual context of AIE, the idea of eight levels of understanding equated to something labeled competence merely means that students should learn the skills and ideas presented in the lessons sufficiently well to pass a paper-and-pencil test. The lessons themselves evidence no discernible developmental logic or order whatsoever. And *readiness* has no more meaning in the program than the unexceptionable fact that lesson 1 is followed by lesson 2. Developmental talk to the contrary, the behavioral emphasis predominates in AIE. Throughout growth is assumed to be precisely controllable, systematic, and progressive by virtue of the lessons.

The use of such language seems to be an attempt to obscure a straightforward process by insisting that the curriculum contains more than just a series of lessons lacking any principle of organization. The language creates the illusion that something more is present, some kind of necessary dynamic that stems from the inherent needs and interests of children. Nothing could be further from the truth. A careful study of the curriculum reveals that AIE reduces art instruction to mechanical procedures that ignore the human aspects of art in the process. Psychological language is used ambiguously to sell a program that is not really as it is made to appear. Given the current demands for a particular approach to curriculum, we wonder whether the program could find acceptance if it were presented simply, directly, and accurately.

The attempt to combine diverse psychological theories under a behaviorist dominance is also evident in the review criteria for *Educational Programs That Work*. Of the eight criteria, only one is related to esthetic understanding: "evidence that the effects are educationally meaningful." But in the context of the other seven critieria, it is likely that "educationally meaningful" is interpreted as increased scores on standardized tests. In fact to strengthen their case, the developrs of AIE are presently constructing and norming paper-and-pencil tests in order to produce evidence that students learn more art (score higher on the tests) when they are taught the AIE curriculum. The rich connotations of "educationally meaningful," with its hints of insight, discovery, and a complex integration of the esthetic, the emotional, the moral, and the cognitive—diverse learning theories—become reduced to a mere, simple measurement standard, to easily quantifiable data from scores on so-called objective tests.

The tests being developed for AIE illustrate just how compelling an influence curriculum form is on a content area. Much that is important, unique, crucial, and special in art is reduced to trivialities. These tests require that students identify or in some cases apply examples of art concepts (*concept* here is used in its peculiar program meaning). For instance, a typical question asks, "Which of the pictures correctly shows parallel lines converging at a point on the eye level (horizon)?" Five pictures follow, just one of which correctly portrays the concept. Another question asks, "The trees in this picture illustrate what artistic principles?: (A) Detail; (B) Symmetry; (C) Grouping; (D) Foreshortening; (E) Conflict."[12] The student looks at the accompanying pictures and selects the correct response. Although these tests are in their fifth revision and are being piloted, it is difficult to imagine that an infinity of revisions could somehow eradicate their irrelevance and render them germane to art education for young children.

For the developers of Art Is Elementary, these tests are a generally happy trade-off between principles and practicalities. While they grant that some things of importance in the arts are lost with a paper-and-pencil testing format, they also believe that a great deal more is gained. What is gained, in their view, is proof that the program works, can be institutionalized, and becomes a means for encouraging the teaching of art. As a program developer told us in an interview:

> I believe that teachers view the subject areas that their kids are tested in all the time as the most important. And when art has never been evaluated—when the teacher's students have never been evaluated as far as their performance in art is concerned—they think it's not really important. (We might add that parents generally agree.) I think it's sad that that's a commentary on our priorities and everything else in the public schools. But I think nonetheless it's true. And I would be willing to have that happen in art just to get more of it going on in the classrooms . . . even though I don't have a very good feeling about that sort of evaluation in the visual arts happening all the time. It gives you a foot in the door.

Hence testing does more than prove that art is a legitimate content area and that the program works—thus facilitating adoption and perhaps funding. It also forces teachers to teach it; it "allows for accountability in art," which is looked on as highly desirable.[13]

ART AND THE ELEMENTARY SCHOOL TEACHER

In some respects the interests of the curriculum developers expressed in Art Is Elementary run contrary to those of the teachers who are to use it. Their intent is to control the teachers' behavior; yet one more area of the curriculum is to be put into the hands of experts who will ensure compliance by establishing standards of accountability.

For many who enjoy teaching art, this curriculum effort is an unwarranted infringement. In part they enjoy teaching art because it is not teaching math or reading; it is a different kind of experience that elicits different kinds of human responses. For these teachers art should not be taught or learned "like any other subject."[14] One such teacher put her position this way: Elementary school children are "too young" for teachers to be concerned about developing in them "sophisticated understanding." They should learn to "enjoy messing with paints and colors" and have an opportunity to "paint and do art and enjoy it — you can get a lot of enjoyment out of it." If they become "a little more observant of things" and "learn to like what they do," it is enough. For this teacher art is important in the curriculum because it allows children to exercise their expressive potential and to find joy doing it. Though she finds much in Art Is Elementary that is helpful, this teacher fears the arrival of the tests. In her view teaching art will not be the same, not nearly so satisfying.

Perhaps many teachers share this dislike of testing in art, but as we have noted in other chapters they will accept it without protest as inevitable if not proper. Elementary school teachers are in a difficult position. They are expected to be able to teach ten or eleven subject areas although in most school districts there is little or no trained help available to them. Art and physical education specialists have long been eliminated to save costs. If these areas are to be taught at all, regular classroom teachers must do it. Those who do not feel comfortable teaching art but who believe it is important find that AIE offers some welcome help. The program is a livable compromise for them. It gives them direction for their teaching and a whole series of easy activities for each lesson. In return they give up their freedom to choose and to develop their own ideas in unique, satisfying ways. For teachers who do not value art except as a time filler or as a reward for good behavior, the requirement of using AIE is a source of irritation because they must now do something formal with art and provide it unwarranted time.

Undoubtedly many of the specific activities in AIE are excellent by themselves, particularly for the novice teacher of art. Where ideas and activities can be plucked out as needed, there is much to be gained. But something happens when the teachers know that their students will be tested. Let us consider one of the typical lessons we observed, lesson 49. The concept to be taught by the lesson is "Colors can be mixed to create specific new colors." The objective to be reached is "The student will demonstrate the ability to predict what specific colors will result when he mixes two given colors."[15] The lesson began with the students gathered closely around the teacher as she reviewed, "Do you remember what primary means?" "Who remembers the secondary colors? Travis, tell me one." "Green." "Do you remember how we make green?" "How do we make purple?" The students seemed eager to respond and generally responded correctly. She then told her students that the other classes she taught this lesson to had mixed orange and green and that this class would mix purple. She called attention to the color they—meaning she—would be mixing by standing up to show the students what she was wearing, a brightly colored outfit composed of various shades of purple. The class

watched as she mixed food coloring into water to make purple. We turn to
our observation notes:

> She began by mixing food coloring into water to make purple. It didn't
> work quite right at first — she got almost black. "What went wrong?"
> "Why?" "Too much blue," they responded. Eventually she got it.
> Then, joy of joys, she brought out a tub of frosting; the kids knew what
> was to follow. She put blue and red into the frosting and mixed it. The
> kids' faces lighted up; some darn near burst with anticipation. Mrs.
> G.: "Is it purple?" She continues to stir. "What kind of purple?" The
> students respond, "Light purple." Mrs. G, "Which is called violet."

The students were then given an assignment. Each received a piece
of paper divided horizontally in half, the upper half of which was also
divided in half. In one of the small boxes of the upper half each student was
to do a drawing using only the three primary colors. In the other small box
they were to do a drawing using the three secondary colors. In the large
box, the bottom half of the paper, they were to do a drawing using all six
colors. As they got started, Mrs. G. urged them to use their "imagina-
tions." While they colored she spread frosting on crackers, stimulating
some students to work very swiftly. As they finished their assignments and
also demonstrated good behavior, she called them up to receive their
"treat," a purple frosting-smeared cracker. The entire lesson took perhaps
twenty to twenty-five minutes; time spent in actual instruction was perhaps
five minutes. The students' drawings seemed to indicate that most of them
understood the concept and had achieved the lesson objective. The
teacher taught the lesson as it is described in Art Is Elementary and did it
well. She seemed to enjoy teaching it, and the students enjoyed doing it.

Following this lesson we spoke with the teacher about it and the
program. She said she selected the lesson we observed because it was the
next one in the program. Her principal decision concerned just which of
the suggested activities to use to accomplish the objective. She commented that currently she is teaching three lessons a week, about twenty to
thirty minutes per lesson. This coincides with the recommendations of
those piloting the tests, who want about an hour and a half of focused art
teaching per week. But she went on to say that she was teaching so many
lessons only because her school started on the concepts late in the year and
was behind in covering all that was necessary for the students to learn. In
effect they were sprinting through the program to make certain the students
were on grade level. Next year, she volunteered, they "will have three

lessons a month." This is, in her opinion, adequate to get her through the year's content.

While Mrs. G. appeared to enjoy what she was doing, her main objective was to get through the lessons so that her students would do well on the tests. However these are not the only educationally detrimental effects of the program. Ultimately, as Mrs. G. herself indicated, progressively less rather than more art instruction will take place. For since the program is a definition of art concept mastery, it is probable that many teachers, like Mrs. G., will spend only enough time teaching art to ensure the minimum mastery required to pass the tests. With AIE, just as we saw in the previous chapter, the technocratic imperative to establish greater control over teacher and student behavior often culminates in a dwindling of both standards of accomplishment and individual efforts, leveling learning to a mind-dulling, mechanically achievable minimum competence.

It would be both unfair and inaccurate to leave the reader with the impression that AIE lacks any educational value whatsoever. Certainly, as we have suggested, used discriminately as an aid to furthering a teacher's own ideas or as a source of activities for the teacher who is unclear about what to do, the AIE compilation can be very helpful. Moreover no matter how trivial most of the concepts and objectives, or how technocratically constrained the curriculum format, some of the lessons are fine and taken by themselves teach important drawing skills. Furthermore any one lesson may inadvertently enhance some desirable learner traits, even fostering values close to the humane aspects of art. To round out our discussion of technocratic-mindedness and art, we will turn to an example that illustrates a positive aspect of the program, its potential for arousing that craft sense of the importance of technique in art.

We observed a sixth-grade class being taught a lesson on the use of shadow to show the time of day. The teacher proceeded just as if he were giving a science lesson. He told the students what they would be doing and then took them outside where they looked at a series of copies of the shadows cast by a basketball standard that he had outlined on the blacktop at different hours of the day. He talked about the appearance of the shadows and asked the students to identify the time of day that had been marked. The students were interested, answered his questions, and seemed to gain an understanding of the relationship between the position of a light source and the shape and position of shadows. They returned to their classroom to observe the shadows made by a lamp variously positioned and to look at the teacher's drawing of shadows coming from a filing cabinet. To end this part of the lesson, the teacher showed prints that illustrated shadow use while he asked the students to estimate the time of the day the artist was trying to depict. The students were next assigned to make pencil sketches of whatever they desired using shadows to show a particular time of day or a light source coming from a particular direction.

It was interesting to observe how intently students worked on their own drawing. They began quickly and continued at their tasks diligently for some twenty minutes, despite the fact that they were a behaviorally "difficult" group, it was late in the school year, and the last period of a long, hot day. Our impression was that these students cared about what they were doing, perhaps partly because the teacher and the lesson activated a sense of craftsmanship. They apparently wanted to see how adept they could be at making a sketch using shadows, and they seemed willing to try hard to produce the correct result. This is a highly desirable outcome of the lesson and fortunately one that the developers, even with their zeal for fitting an art program into a technocratic form, seem to value. The suggested evaluation for the lesson is "The student's work, his verbal responses to questions, and the contributions he makes to general discussions are all ample evidence that the objective has been achieved."[16] Encouraging ideals of craftsmanship in the young is an educational virtue, important for all learning and particularly germane to an art curriculum. Though it is perhaps not clearly emphasized, this sense of the importance of craftsmanship is present to a degree in several of the lessons in AIE, in some of the teacher in-service work we observed, and undoubtedly in some teachers' instruction. For instance we observed this teacher explain to a couple of interested students with pride how he had made his chalkboard sketch of a filing cabinet and its shadow. Perhaps this illustrates how a curriculum form can be temporarily breached. During these times students and teacher are involved in the serious and satisfying project of developing their capacities.

The benefits of the program, although peripheral, are educationally important. For the experienced sixth-grade teacher we observed, who acknowledged his ignorance of the arts, AIE is better than his previous approach to teaching art. Nevertheless these positive aspects are limited by the pervasive form of the curriculum. For example his primary concern was whether the teachers of the preceding elementary grades would use the program just as designed so that he would be able to teach exactly what the students were supposed to learn in the sixth grade. We sense that AIE provides this teacher with a convenient, easy to implement set of activities that absolves him of any need to think beyond the specific lessons he must teach. From his point of view, if teachers will only follow the program set forth by the experts, instruction will be easy and effective, all students will pass the competency exams, and art education will be well and painlessly taken care of. In just this way the program, like the others analyzed, seduces practitioners into greater reliance on technocratic-mindedness for defining and solving education (and cultural) problems.

CONCLUSION

In this chapter our aim has been to disclose how even art education, the one realm of study that would seem immune from the grip of techno-cratic-mindedness, today falls victim to it nevertheless. We have argued that the current cultural understanding of the educational legitimacy or value of any content area taught in the public schools is almost exclusively determined by the criteria of technocratic adequacy. We have used the topic of art education, ostensibly the most unlikely of conforming subjects, to illustrate our case. The ironic upshot of the technocratic imperative applied to art education is that the unique values associated with art lose so much vigor, become so adulterated by the dictate to conform or perish, that they are essentially eradicated. It is vexing to realize that all of our educational values, most particularly including those special to art, have been and are being altered, adulterated, and reduced in order to fit content into the technocratic curriculum form. We must view with disquiet the spectacle of art educators trying to justify their educationally meaningful subject as just one more component in the overall effort of enhancing narrow skills while helping produce politically stable citizens.

Chapter 5

Careers and Consciousness: Alternative Education in Secondary Schools

Schooling of course does not end with childhood. Secondary education continues the preparation for life begun in elementary school, and a technocratic outlook still structures the work of teachers and students. However, the students' characteristics change. Growth signals increasing potential to think critically, to understand abstract ideas, and to resist doing things merely because they are required. Adolescence creates special concerns for parents and educators because young persons are now developmentally equipped to refuse to participate in supposedly essential activities.

This chapter concerns those young adults who do exercise the power to say "No," who reject the value of the typical high school experience. Though the great majority of students accept schooling as it is and go along, a fairly large minority seem either unwilling or unable to do so. This presents educators (and parents) with the challenge of keeping them in school until they graduate and can move on to jobs or further education. Somehow these young folk must be convinced that staying in school is worthwhile. This is crucial because technocratic culture relies on public schooling to nurture a vision of social life as a happy harmony in which each person is fitted for and provided a useful role to perform; a place for everyone, everyone in her place. In this desired society, the allocation of roles, from dentist to gravedigger, is considered fair because it is based on schooling.

A person who has been graduated from high school is trusted to have acquired the dispositions, values, and skills needed for surviving in our society. A high school diploma is the credential that certifies the bearer fit to inhabit a useful vocational slot—secretary, police officer, miner, waiter —or permits access to further training and the more specific credentials required for working as teacher, violinmaker, radiologist, or beautician. Inculcating the disposition to believe in the necessity of getting the credential and of undergoing the process that bestows it—schooling—is therefore essential to culture; schooling is the fundamental rite of passage for youth in technocratic society and our chief means of ensuring social harmony.

From this point of view, not surprisingly, young folk asserting their unwillingness to fit in pose an apparent threat to social harmony. Parents and teachers suppose that these adolescents have failed to internalize proper values because they do not wish to stay in school. These seeming misfits are considered potentially dangerous, not in a political sense, as radicals, but as direct threats to safety and property. They are looked on as the next generation of thieves and drug users or at best as the ne'er-do-wells who will crowd the welfare roles, chronically unable to provide for themselves. As we will show, this is a misperception, for these young people do indeed hold the desired values although they cannot see the relevance of high school to finding a place and fitting in. They believe they can do that very nicely, thank you, without the bother of high school.

During the past fifteen years, school systems throughout the United States have responded to these students by creating alternative programs. Such programs are touted as offering a different kind of education, some-thing more relevant, more in line with adolescents' interests and needs. We studied one of these programs, EBCE (Experienced Based Career Education). EBCE is a national program whose developers claim is now in over six hundred high schools.[1] It draws its content from a range of career and service experiences available in a community. It presumes that getting and keeping a job is the chief interest of turned-off adolescents who, if offered a program that helps them explore jobs and prepare for work, will assuredly become turned-on students.

EBCE students and teachers, like others in alternative programs, believe they are participating in a unique educational experience. In this chapter we will explore how EBCE does and does not differ from the regular school program. To anticipate somewhat, our general conclusion is that while educational means may differ in EBCE, the outcomes do not. More importantly, the program extends the power of the school to blunt incipient critical-mindedness by redirecting it onto pathways that assure system maintenance. Hence what appears to be a radical education is in fact a conservative one aimed at achieving proper adjustment to work interest values.

COMMUNITY AND STUDENTS

EBCE is based on the supposition that direct involvement in the study of various careers will provide a person with the knowledge, skills, and attitudes required to live the good and successful life. For EBCE the range of jobs available in a community corresponds to what is worth knowing. Thus by participating in and studying local occupations, high school students can be educated. This is the heart of the alternative idea for EBCE and its basic principle of program construction.

EBCE makes an interesting distinction between involvement in the broader activities of a community and participation in the community through work. High school students, of course, participate in a variety of community activities including part-time jobs. EBCE, however, recognizes only one aspect of community: its professional and semiprofessional jobs, activities not directly accessible to high school students. A study of community, then, does not include learning about its political, social, or cultural activities. Rather the idea of community is stringently narrowed to mean merely available careers. The point seems clear: Full community membership requires holding a full-time job. Therefore learning the attitudes, skills, and knowledge necessary for securing a job is the purpose of school, and, by extension, the most critical part of life. The underlying message of this narrow conception is that schooling and learning are not for understanding the community but for being fitted into it.

A look at some of the characteristics EBCE students share provides insight into the values and attitudes that schools promote. According to the EBCE director interviewed, without the program "about one-third of the students would probably leave school" although the remaining two-thirds would likely stay because "they're neat kids" who are nevertheless "frustrated by the conventional curriculum." One reason for this frustration, according to one of the EBCE teachers, is that some of the "very, very bright students are bored with school." Though turned off by the regular program, they "come in here specifically knowing what they want to do, where they want to go." All the EBCE students, no matter what their academic abilities, were dissatisfied with the standard program. To use their favorite word, it was "boring."

A second characteristic of these students is interesting because it conflicts with expectations. Along with their more contented peers, EBCE students held that securing a job was the essential reason for completing high school, but in contrast they viewed the standard curriculum as valueless, as nothing more than empty credits to accumulate. Thus while acknowledging that a high school diploma was needed for entree to full social life, they denied that there was any relationship whatsoever between the content they were required to learn and the work adults do. These young people were cynical about schooling; they accepted society's shibboleth that it was necesary to graduate from high school in order to earn money, but they rejected belief in any other benefits of learning.

Many EBCE students also shared difficulty in conforming to school rules. As one student confided, "I fought strict rules and had trouble . . . because I did the opposite of what people told me." EBCE, however, worked for her because she "had the freedom to choose," she said, "and when I make my own commitments, I keep them." Students needing a different arrangement of their time and a different kind of supervision, with some freedom to move outside the confines of the campus, liked EBCE.

A fourth characteristic of EBCE students is that they did not participate in the social life of the school. This is a point of some importance, for it is widely recognized that such participation has great holding power. As one EBCE teacher said, "I see them not getting in. They don't go to assemblies. They don't go to football or basketball games. . . . I'm sure there's not one kid in here that went to the junior prom." They were on the fringe of the student body, having segregated themselves from the mainstream, sharing the same campus but not the same social life as their peers. An EBCE student we talked with dismissed the value of standard classes by deriding their heavy social emphasis: "All we ever talked about was who sits by who." Regular classes held nothing for her because she was not part of these discussions. Neither this young woman nor her EBCE fellows saw the classroom as essential for making new friends or contacts with the opposite sex. Such an outlook, of course, means the typical program will be just that much more difficult to endure. It is quite a different chore to do tedious work as a member of a social group, sharing the tedium with friends, commiserating together, than it is to do it alone, isolated, an outsider. The students who come to EBCE reminded us of those workers who see no purpose in their toil and do not enjoy the people they work with but are trapped because they must have that paycheck. EBCE offers such students a way to escape their situation while virtually ensuring that they will not question the conventions of contemporary social life.

In sum EBCE students seemed to be saying that they wanted to become working members of the community. They wanted to find the best sorts of jobs, but they also hated having to stay in the regular program in order to get them. They were not interested in the social life of the school and, importantly, saw the school's purpose as strictly vocational. And while some of them still had to learn dependability and the importance of hard work, they also needed a different setting in order for this aim to be accomplished. EBCE seems to offer such a setting and in the process is able to bring socially marginal adolescents back into the mainstream.

THE PROGRAM

Keeping these student characteristics in mind, let us turn to the key organizational specifics of EBCE. At the center of the program are entities called *resources*. Resources are individuals in the community who are willing to have students work with them for several weeks. In the EBCE program we studied, students chose from a range of placements that included the local zoo, a number of businesses, the airlines, a school for emotionally handicapped children, a funeral home, and local hospitals. The student selects one or two placements each semester and plans a project to do as part of the job experience. According to EBCE literature, "Students plan and carry out their learning through individual projects, using goals and evaluation criteria they help specify."[2] The focus on student projects purportedly helps distinguish EBCE from vocational training. This is important to the program developers who urge that in EBCE careers are used to enrich school learning. They insist that EBCE is not vocational education, which in their view means both specific job training and fostering what used to be called "industrial intelligence," that is, the skills, attitudes, and values of good workers.

The central person in helping the student plan the project is the teacher, renamed "learning coordinator." The learning coordinator's role

— which will be discussed in greater detail shortly — is substantially different from the typical high school teacher's. Learning coordinators help students select a placement and plan a project. They also teach language skills, provide personal counseling, and supervise academic programs. In the process of doing these things, they generally become friends with their students. Each learning coordinator supervises from fifteen to twenty students every semester. Students must check in daily with the learning coordinator and meet for an extended period each week when progress is assessed and problems addressed.

The projects students do emphasize the usual academic skills. All projects minimally consist of a written report, but they often contain something additional, perhaps a demonstration, a slide show, or the construction of a model. One student, for instance, whose placement was with the zoo, designed cages for small zoo animals. He presented these designs as part of his project along with the written description of his placement experiences. For the most part, the projects are technical in nature. They describe how to do something and indicate which work-related skills and attitudes have to be developed.

JAN: LIFE AS CAREER

We can best illustrate the power of vocations to keep students in school and the kinds of activities EBCE promotes by looking at a student we shall call Jan. Jan is an attractive, intelligent senior in her second EBCE year. She has worked in a variety of placements since joining the program—a hospital, a court of law, a physical therapy practice, and a small business. Jan believes in EBCE. Like many others in it, she found regular high school boring and mostly useless, but she feels EBCE is helping her to learn the really important things.

We talked with Jan several times during the year, once in a formal interview that included the resource she was working with at the time. Since the resources are responsible for guiding the work, their attitudes and values are important influences on what students may learn in a placement. The resource we interviewed has participated in EBCE for about three years. She is the owner-manager of a small business and commented several times on how much she enjoys working with high school students. She feels that she has something important to offer them and that they are helpful in running her business. Her role, as she understands it, is to provide students like Jan with the personal support they need to feel good about themselves and to give them an opportunity to learn "how the real world functions." Her general attitude toward life is clear. As she related, she works long hours to make her business succeed and believes that if students adopt the same attitude, are willing to put out the necessary effort, they too will be successful. "It isn't easy to make a go of it in today's world, but everyone can succeed if they'll work hard enough." Success for her is tied to the ability to make money, and she is certain she can help students learn what this takes.

Jan has been a good worker, responsible and reliable. While at this placement, she was required to evaluate a Christmas display, prepare for a Valentine's Day sale, and lend a hand wherever needed. The typical work Jan reported doing involved unpacking and labeling merchandise, waiting on customers, and taking phone orders. Certainly these activities are not unpleasant, but they are also routine. Furthermore, we must ask, how are they educative?

Jan's project for this placement was a written report that described and evaluated a Christmas display that the store had prepared for a customer. She detailed the creation of the display and suggested how the process might be improved upon. Jan told us that she generally liked to do something more than just a written report, such as a slide presentation, but that this time she simply did not feel like doing any additional work.

Her attitude about involvement in the placements seemed mature and probably exemplifies the kind of caution the EBCE program wants to foster. She commented, for instance, that while her work in the small business was not one of the more interesting placements she had had, it was still all right. Even though Jan does not anticipate ever owning or operating a small business, she saw value in learning about its operations because, as she put it, "You never really know what's going to happen in life."

In our various conversations with Jan, a couple of concerns seemed ever present: whether her current placement might be something she would like as a career, and her social life. She seemed to have learned well the importance of getting the right job, of finding the right fit, whatever that job or fit might be. Though she is bright and perceptive, vocational and personal issues dominated her thinking to the exclusion of any cultural or political interests. Getting a job and having friends is what life is all about for her. Education is nothing more than what one has to do to get a job, and good education is active, pleasant, general vocational preparation. As long as the goal of a proper fit is being pursued, and because she recognizes the importance of luck in finding it, Jan has high tolerance for vocational experiences that turn out to be off the mark. She has faith that eventually a fit will be found and education will have paid off.

Jan does not allow that there might be anything more to education than the search for a vocation. The values of the workplace are also hers and have been reinforced by schooling. The understandings she seeks and gets offered are technical in nature, primarily skills: how to sell to customers, how to organize a display, how to run a small business, and so forth. Her EBCE activities lack the qualities that characterize liberal education. That is, her schooling serves ends that are extrinsic to education and are concerned essentially, or even exclusively, with vocational preparation. Vocation as goal and as means has so effectively channeled Jan's dissatisfaction with school that it is now remembered only as something "boring." She has little understanding of why she was dissatisfied and, more importantly, no comprehension that in leaving the regular program for EBCE she gave up access to the knowledge and discipline that might have helped her develop this understanding. The school, in the name of serving her needs and interests, effectively denied Jan the opportunity of becoming educated.

DIFFERENCES IN PROGRAMS

We have noted that for many students, perhaps most, the purpose of education is to get a job. We have discussed how this belief is used to keep students in school through programs that play directly to that outlook. Students in such programs believe they are getting a different kind of education. Now it remains for us to examine this belief and program assertion in regard to EBCE.

Alternative curricula, by definition, promise some kind of relief for students and teachers who are uncomfortable with the various constraints of standard schooling such as fifty-minute periods spent sitting in classrooms. Differences are stressed to help establish program identity and a sense of belonging; "we" are not as "they" are. The differences between EBCE and the regular school program seem so striking at first glance that it is difficult to imagine any similarities other than superficial ones: There are teachers and students, students receive credit toward graduation for work done, teachers give grades.

In our earlier description of EBCE, we pointed out some distinctions between it and the regular school program. For example, students spend most of their day away from the school, and the resources are the chief instructors. This section examines EBCE's uniqueness in three areas: teacher role, teacher-student relationships, and teaching content. We selected these three areas because they were important points of focus in our analysis of rationalized curricula (e.g., GEMS, IGE). EBCE is not, however, highly rationalized. In fact for a variety of reasons, most high school curricula at present are not though they are becoming more so. But uniqueness notwithstanding, those students who do not have or properly express technocratic values need the remediation that programs like EBCE offer. The medicine is different, but the effect is the same.

EBCE teachers do not behave like other teachers; if they did many of their students would leave the program. As learning coordinators EBCE teachers see themselves as "facilitators" who are "concerned with getting the kids turned on and responsible for themselves so that they will pick it up and go." Discipline is not a problem because the students themselves and the resources take care of it. Learning coordinators do not give assignments in the usual sense but meet with students and make contracts for the work to be done. They are more concerned about the processes of learning, the "experiencing" that occurs, than about achieving specific learning outcomes. They try to give their students freedom to "explore, explore, explore" believing that such freedom is the cause of learning and far "more beneficial than taking courses just to fill time slots" — their outlook on the regular school program. In short they are humanistic teachers in the best sense of the term, those who nurture, facilitate, stimulate, and guide learning.

Learning coordinators spend much of every day in meetings, for the most part in groups or individually with the fifteen to twenty students assigned to them. They also, though less frequently, spend time with the resources and the parents. And while the resources are held in high regard —"These community people are terrific!"—nevertheless learning coordinators devote time to ensuring that resources will not see themselves as formal instructors who must teach the students something specific. Another important segment of the day is given over to conferring with parents and keeping them informed, tasks the learning coordinators take seriously and work hard at. One parent we observed came in to discuss what he might do to help his son graduate, a goal all three shared. To graduate the student needed to earn additional credits. Among the three of them—student, parent, and learning coordinator—a scheme was developed so that the necessary number of credits could be earned if the boy completed his prior contract, did six book reports, and helped his father with the books of the family business. To underscore the importance of getting this work done, the teacher reminded the father of what he already knew: His son would be seriously limited in the marketplace if he did not finish school.

The relationships learning coordinators have with students are marked by friendship and caring. The students say that unlike other teachers, those in EBCE are trustworthy allies who, moreover, provide levels of support and recognition normally denied them in school. The students feel there is harmony between their interests and those of the learning coordinators, a shared feeling in fact; "We are," said a learning coordinator, "with the students working toward a common goal." Friendship is a powerful incentive for students to do well since of course friends wish to please one another. By the same token, it encourages learning coordinator flexibility; they commonly give students second chances. In contrast, where regular teachers are not generally seen as friends, rejection of school requirements is easy, and EBCE students did just that. In EBCE, program and people are so closely identified it is difficult to reject one without rejecting the other; friendship with learning coordinators comes only with involvement in the program.

Both students and learning coordinators establish the agendas for the required weekly conferences. We observed one meeting where the topic, proposed by the student, was how to organize a report on a placement experience. The teacher listened attentively, asked questions, and gave suggestions. The quality of this interaction was typical of EBCE, respectful and supportive. The student left this meeting with a clearer understanding of what he needed to do to get his credit. In another meeting the learning coordinator gently reminded two young women of their past failures in the program and urged them to do better with their new placement. The message sent was clear: You've goofed up but can do the work if you'll try, and I'll help all I can. Other topics of discussion included grades, problems with placements or resources, possible future placements, and personal family problems.

The learning coordinators are quite definite about not being content specialists. They do not teach history, English, or biology per se; rather their concern is with what they call "life skills." Life skills appear to be of two kinds: so-called processes, which are generic intellectual skills such as some kind of general problem-solving and general decision-making ability, and the skills of basic literacy such as reading and computing. Concern for life skills is crucial because learning coordinators cannot be expert in the variety of work-related activities for which their students receive academic (graduation) credits. That is, they cannot attend in any sophisticated fashion to what is involved in, for example, running a flower shop. But they can claim expertise in the realm of guiding life skills. Furthermore the learning coordinators claim that not only do students forget most of the content they learn in school, but that this content has little utility even if recalled. What has real utility, they assert, are those life skills that can supposedly be used in a variety of work settings regardless of any differences in the nature of the work. Thus one of the EBCE teachers could say, "It probably isn't anything at all like the content they would learn in regular courses, but I think that they learn the same skills."

The emphasis on life skills, on process and basic literacy, establishes the educational legitimacy of a wide range of activities usually considered outside the school's domain. In EBCE all sanctioned activities are thought of as equally beneficial. Problem solving, for instance, is understood as a single, unitary process that can be learned in any setting whatsoever. This outlook frustrates subject matter teachers who occasionally express displeasure that credit in biology, say, is given for activity only remotely connected with the discipline. To such displeasure one learning coordinator responded in interview, "When a kid earns a biology credit here . . . I would say to the subject matter teacher, 'For this particular student, this was a reasonable biology experience. With your textbook up there and all that nonsense, unless these kids are going to be scientists, then I would say your textbook is ridiculous.'"

This defense effectively reduces the importance of developing disciplined knowledge. In effect what students will do is taken to be what they ought to do. The play to immediate vocational interests, the presumed glamour of a particular career, or the promise of financial reward reinforces what students already believe: The disciplines are irrelevant and the only knowledge worth having is that which pays off in dollars and cents. The students and EBCE teachers seem to hold that experience of any kind that has a biological or historical or political science flavor, however trivial or remote, is as important and as valuable as any other activity in these areas and should be awarded credit accordingly. Lacking respect for disciplined knowledge, the EBCE student, like most of his peers in the regular school program, sees no value in general education. The worship of vocation as both the means and end of education excludes studying those content areas most likely to develop cultural understanding and personal or social insight. Rarely is even a modicum of attention paid to the humanities or the social and natural sciences, for clearly these areas have little career utility. The student is left with an education focused on processes concerned either with technical, often business-related matters, such as running an airport, or with solving the personal problems that may interfere with graduation. One important result of this emphasis is to discourage the idea of citizens as participants who strive to understand political-social issues and to encourage the model of citizen as complacent consumer.

The differences in teacher role, teacher-student relationships, and the use of content create an abundance of problems for learning coordinators because for all the differences, they still have to work under institutional constraints and in accord with district rules. These problems denote the tensions that arise in the gray areas where EBCE and the regular school program must adjust to each other, and they point up some of the difficulties of working within an institution ostensibly to change it. A program that is too different, with teachers perceived as uncooperative, can expect a short life in spite of the accurate claims of alternative school proponents that such programs generally pay for themselves by increasing student attendance.

At times the learning coordinator role and institutional expectations clash. It is, as one teacher commented, a "kind of schizophrenic thing." Mediating between students' wants and institutional demands—which the students have in some measure rejected—is a difficult, precarious undertaking. Standards and friendship do not always mix happily. The teachers are helped by their student friends, who, to a degree, understand the problem of dual commitments. They believe that as far as possible friendship will prevail over the institution. There are, however, minimal institutional requirements that cannot be disregarded without jeopardizing a teacher's employment, a program's survival, or a student's graduation.

This "schizophrenic thing" is partially, though unintentionally, eased by obscuring standards. While traditional notions of academic excellence do not and cannot be applied, it is also the case that new, appropriate standards have not been developed. In their stead is the understanding that students should follow through on the commitments they negotiated with their learning coordinator; that is, they must do some schoollike activities and demonstrate the desired attitudes. Thus they should always be on time, spend a certain number of hours on the job, and the like in order to satisfy an intuitive sense of the minimum effort necessary for receiving credit. And doing schoollike activities usually means writing a report on virtually anything the student wishes.

Standards are further obscured by the emphasis on process skills. After all, what marks progress in decision making or in problem solving? Appraisal in this realm depends heavily on the quality of the student-learning coordinator relationship. Evaluation is also complicated by the fact that the learning coordinators cannot possibly be expert in the content of every placement experience. Nevertheless, for credit purposes, judgments about the placements must be made. Learning coordinators necessarily have to rely on student self-reports and on the evaluations of the resources. Hence students and resources share responsibility with the learning coordinators for the institutional task of grading, a process of diffusion and compromise that blurs a sense of standards.

Ironically, while what may receive credit is considerably broadened in EBCE, it still must be accounted for in traditional subject matter categories. This presents the learning coordinators with the problem of packaging a student's experiences for graduation. Packaging decisions center on two general considerations: the nature of the placement experience (does it logically fall into a category—English, social studies?) and which credits a student needs to fulfill district graduation requirements. Students in the same placement might therefore receive credit in different subject matter categories. For example, English or social studies or health credit might be given for work done in an agency serving children. To get the desired fit between graduation requirements and student activity, the learning coordinators admit they "bend the content" and constantly push up against the boundaries of schooling.

EBCE is viewed by friend and foe as a strong, even a fundamental challenge to the present system. And it is either just tolerated or lauded because it is committed to the ideal of every student's right to an appropriate education. However, in the interest of refusing to take things at face value, we think it is fair to question whether EBCE is as radically different as is claimed. Does it in fact challenge the system? Are students' interests served? And is it education?

A ROSE BY ANY NAME

While we acknowledge the importance of the difference between EBCE and regular schooling, we shall nevertheless show that on several significant considerations, EBCE differs not at all. We contend, to the contrary, that although EBCE does offer variations on the *means* of schooling, the outcomes it produces—its actual effects on students—are essentially those of the regular program. This is not to gainsay the educational value of some of the differences in means. For surely establishing mutually respectful associations with teachers and other adults gives promise of a better education.

A look at EBCE's emphasis on "life skills," however, discloses an important instance of similarity with regular schooling, in this case with elementary education. Life skills refer to basic forms of literacy and of problem-solving/decision-making processes thought necessary for survival, applicable to virtually any situation a human might find herself in and learnable through any content because the processes signify a general unitary ability. Yet interestingly, developing these very skills and enhancing ability with these processes are central tasks of elementary schooling. EBCE differs only on broadness of means, claiming that decision-making or problem-solving ability per se can be learned in any setting whatsoever —working at the zoo, for the Bureau of Mines, or in a flower shop. Just why EBCE has to repeat the aims of elementary schooling is an important question on which we shall try to shed some light.

Our interviews and observations show that students in EBCE get considerable opportunity to improve their reading and writing. Indeed the learning coordinators work hard to ensure progress in these areas by requiring the completion of a number of reading-writing projects for each career placement. But the goals of this special concern are the same kind that guide the teaching-learning of reading and writing in the elementary school. In this endeavor EBCE evidently holds that the content is irrelevant for learning or refining literacy because only skill acquisition counts. Reading is emphasized as a means of getting information, for collecting data. EBCE students, for instance, would be required to read the business section of the newspaper to find information for a project report but not serious literature or historical and political documents. This stress narrows reading from a pleasurable activity enjoyable in its own right or from a means for critical understanding to a mere skill for gathering data to meet the requirements of a specific task. Likewise EBCE students write primarily in order to describe the "how to's" or "how it works" of processes and mechanisms but not often to express feelings, perceptions, attitudes, or complex ideas.

The focus is similar for the other "life skills" students are to acquire in EBCE. The problem-solving and decision-making skills taught are directly work-related. Of course problems arising in occupations are important, but that exclusive concern diminishes a sense of what is or ought to be problematic in life. Moreover, while problem solving may perhaps be broadly understood as a general ability, it is by no means obvious that skillful problem solving in one occupation readily transfers to others as, for instance, from operating a small business to getting a car to run or from finding oil shale to housing elephants. Actually, in respect to the abilities enhanced, it makes a difference whether a student works at a flower shop or at the Bureau of Mines. Although this is acknowledged, problem solving in the EBCE occupations calls for precise technical information and relevant methods of evaluation specific to those areas of work, that is, a variety of special procedures. EBCE, however, disregards this fact and promotes two reductions. On the one hand, it reduces all problem-solving methods to those that work for technical issues and perplexities. On the other hand, it claims that problem solving is a unitary process. This is a striking example of technocratic-mindedness. Once again we find a current educational program thoroughly imbued with technocratic values.

The structure of EBCE promotes another technocratic value: reliance on experts. Characteristically students participate in a placement by doing a few of the less technical aspects of a job but chiefly by observing experts doing the more technical ones. This is of course an entirely appropriate set-up. The neophyte observes the experts solving job-engendered problems. Jan, the young woman discussed earlier, was confined to observing in her placement with a physical therapist. Nevertheless she believed she learned how the therapist decided on treatment for each patient, that is, she learned the therapist's problem-solving procedures. Surely Jan learned even more forcefully that it takes experts to solve problems and that life is best lived in accord with their dictates. Furthermore the EBCE view that problem-solving and decision-making skills are all of a piece, that they generalize across occupations and throughout life, that learning these skills *is* education, that success in business is proof of the pudding, masks the limitations of relying on experts and on this notion of problem solving in our struggles to live a meaningful life. It suppresses learning to call things into question, to be critical, probing, broadly reflective—precisely the hopes and virtues of a liberal or general education. Like the children at Flowing Brook, EBCE students are trained to be reliable workers; they are not being educated to become free.

EBCE teachers also aim at inculcating or firming up reliable worker qualities such as punctuality, following directions, deference, honesty, and the like. These too are judged by the learning coordinators and figured into students' grades. As one learning coordinator put it, "When kids come back from their placements, I say, 'Well, what do you think you really got out of that?' They say, 'Well, I learned how to manage my own time. . . .'" They learn, in other words, to exhibit promptness and other qualities bespeaking an efficient worker. The resources themselves stress these values in their job performance requirements and by serving as role models, as successful persons for having internalized the approved qualities. In chapter 3 we argued that fostering good worker characteristics was a central aim of elementary education; present analysis shows that EBCE accords the same status to this aim.

With respect to educational means, EBCE learning coordinators, like elementary school teachers, lack a content specialty and give grades in virtually every content area. Moreover they too believe that teaching through love is more likely to get results than any other means. As one EBCE teacher observed, "I play the role of substitute mother. In some cases even more than that." Other means are not prevalent because the power relationship between learning coordinators and students is thought to be radically different in EBCE: "You really have very little power to do things to kids," we were advised. Hence although EBCE is a secondary school program, it shares with elementary schooling both the aim of developing desired attitudes, values, and skills and a preference for nurturing by means of love.

Elementary education aims persist because a portion of EBCE students, those potential dropouts for whom the program was created, presumably did not learn the lessons in elementary school. Previous schooling was somehow ineffective for them. Yet, ironically, it is not generally true that they do not possess the desired qualities, but rather the problem is that they do not express them appropriately, that is, in ways leading to graduation. For instance, a student may never be late to a part-time job (and many hold them) but frequently tardy to school. At issue is the possession of these values as they relate to schooling on the questionable presumption that as they are evidenced in school so will they be in the workplace — late to school, ergo, late to work. Time and again in our interviews and conversations, EBCE people urged that without the approved qualities students could not survive—get a decent job—in the adult world. Therefore in spite of holding down part-time jobs, EBCE students received additional elementary education in an effort to stamp in the right values. Revealingly, what was deemed necessary for the one-third or so identified as lacking in this education, and as likely to fail in life, established the character of the program in toto, for all students, even those who had evidently mastered their lessons and had the values. For these students EBCE was an easy, comparatively enjoyable way of getting credits minus the hassles accompanying participation in the regular school program.

The apparent fact that most EBCE students already possess the right qualities, though perhaps do not demonstrate them in preferred ways or to the desired degree in school, suggests that there must be other reasons for the potency of the survival argument for parents, teachers, and students. One reason is surely the presumed equivalence between school and work mentioned earlier. While clearly problematic, this identity, which ignores differences in motivation, is unquestioned; it seems to be a cultural given. A second reason is our taken-for-granted acceptance of credentialing, itself a facet of the technocratic belief in the necessity of social hierarchy capped by experts. High school graduation then is an early stage in the process of forming or maintaining the hierarchy by providing a means for assigning places: up a step with a diploma, down two without one. This practice is accepted as the way things work best, as required for making the good life. Even when the practice seems dubious, when, for example, a clearly incompetent, even undeserving person gets a position solely by virtue of having a diploma or degree, it is taken as correct and inevitable, a feature of the system not open to challenge. It is simply understood that a high school diploma, whether or not it has anything to do with learning, is necessary for finding a place in the work force.

The diploma is earned by accumulating a predetermined number of credits in selected content areas. Credit is awarded on a formula that says spending a given amount of time in a class doing passable work equals a certain amount of credit. Time equals credit; therefore time equals learning. But no one knows what, if anything, the graduated student has learned, and with EBCE students it is even difficult to tell how much time has been spent where. However, these questions do not arise and hence do not matter, and EBCE students and learning coordinators know this; what counts is possessing a diploma. Employers use the diploma to screen potential employees while teachers remind students of this practice in order to keep them in school. The school serves the employer, and the employer's practice helps legitimate the school. In an economic system that regarded credentials as unimportant but awarded opportunity on demonstrated ability, EBCE students would likely fare as well as in the current credentialing system. The diploma may have rather little to do with learning, but it certainly has much to do with gaining access to earning, a fact EBCE students are not permitted to forget.

The fact that alternative programs like EBCE must be established should prompt raising normative questions about schooling: What is it good for? However, this does not appear to be the case. To the contrary, creating alternative programs seems to inhibit such questioning. Primarily this is a result of the way the programs are developed. Typically, when the number of poorly functioning students gets to the point at which questions might be raised about a school's effectiveness, a system-protective mechanism kicks into operation. First commonalities among the deviant students are identified. (Up to this point deviance was treated in isolated, individual cases.) Then students are grouped by their common problems and needs. These are always identified as some kind of deficiency in the students; they lack basic skills or the right attitudes or appropriate values or have some such shortcoming. Students are neatly labeled; their problems have been, so to speak, assigned to them, like homework. Significantly, problems or needs are never located in the structure of things, in some aspect of the schools such as its roles or content, but always within the individual student. Next programs are set up in order to keep these groups in school so that attendance percentages can be maintained at the level of community expectation. If the programs work, normative questions remain suppressed and possibly healthy value confrontations between school and community do not get aired; if the programs prove ineffective, new ones will be trotted out posthaste.

EBCE students rejected the regular school program as boring and irrelevant to their vocational interests. They wanted a program more responsive to their needs that would give them a diploma with as little work and fuss as possible. And it seems as if they got what they wanted. Serving their school time is made at least tolerable, and they can feel a sense of accomplishment for having apparently beaten the system. For those willing to stick with the program, there is the promise of a payoff in future jobs with former EBCE students who have made it providing vivid reminders of the possibility. By virtue of this alternative curriculum, students who did not fit in now have a place, and the system is understood to be doing its job.

The eventual results are tragic because the practice enhances technocratic society's capacity to sustain the belief that an individual's interests are identical with the system's. That illusion vitiates the inherently desirable tension between individual and collective. Schooling contributes significantly to this process by defining such tension as aberrance needing the treatment of a new alternative program that will ensure a smooth transition to adult life. The aberrant learn to fit in—rather, are fitted in—all the while thinking their uniqueness is being honored by the special treatment they receive. Alternatives like EBCE unfortunately obscure the acute differences between the values of school and the values of work, making it appear as if schooling is exactly equivalent to working. Hence our work interest predominates, constraining fuller expression of our communication and emancipation interests while education becomes essentially vocational preparation, and its value per se is eliminated from schooling. But it is crucial that distinctions between school and work be vitally maintained, for without them the emancipatory potential of education gets hopelessly lost in the service of economic and cultural reproduction.

It is also tragic that because EBCE students are led to believe their education is totally unlike that provided in the regular program, they think they have foiled the system and are free, independent masters of their own destinies. The program prevents them from seeing that the results are exactly the same. They—like all students—are in school to acquire the skills and attitudes needed in the world of work and one way or another, they are going to get them—in elementary school for most, through alternatives for others. The delusion fostered here points up a pernicious paradox common to many alternative programs. Teachers recognizing the delusion nevertheless must acknowledge that without it their students would not complete school; hence necessity forces them both to perpetuate a false belief and to pervert their students' education thereby. For students it virtually guarantees willing service to the very system they resisted and thought themselves capable of manipulating. In EBCE their elementary education is completed; they become what they are supposed to be, good consumers, good workers, and citizens who value things being just as they are.

HUMANISTIC AND TRADITIONAL TEACHING

Recently the goal of producing emancipatory education has been associated with teaching methods some educators have labeled humanistic. Humanistic teaching is usually contrasted with the conservative aims and means of so-called traditional teaching and is considered to provide a critique and negation of the educational (and political) status quo. Thus traditional teachers are looked on as valuing subject matter and skill competence above all else, as taking the logic of the disciplines rather than the needs of students as the basis for curriculum organization, and as relying on lectures, drill, workbook assignments, and objective examinations for preferred instructional means. From the humanistic standpoint, traditional teachers are seen as cold, uncaring, and devoted to stifling educational and social change. By contrast humanistic teachers perceive themselves as valuing individual needs, feelings, and desires above all else, as intimately involved with helping the young work through their developmental problems, as given to teaching by activity, interaction, and discovery, and devoted to openness, experimentation, change, and the new. From the traditional point of view, humanistic teachers are soft, anti-intellectual, and socially irresponsible.

The comparisons certainly tend to be caricatures and misleading. Nevertheless, because EBCE teachers are humanistic in the best sense of the term, they are aligned with the teaching that encourages critical-mindedness and promotes other causes often considered educationally radical — student independence, community involvement, freedom, and the like. But in EBCE such causes, as we have shown, are so circumscribed by the needs of cultural and economic reproduction that student independence and community involvement mean getting a job and going to work on time. It is indeed sad to realize that the illusions of freedom, involvement, and independence come so dear, for they are bought at the cost of the disciplined knowledge that above all other means can lead to critical understanding.

This does not deny the possibility that EBCE helps some students develop critical-mindedness or meaningful community participation. However, in our view the program more likely thwarts the possibility because friendship, love, and "experiencing" in school settings without an emphasis on securing critical understanding smother instead of foster emancipatory struggles. Traditional methods or humanistic teaching, alternative education or regular school program, individualized or standard grouping techniques — no matter the differences, the stronger similarities leave the poignant message that schooling is primarily dedicated to fitting the young into politically safe, corporately beneficial roles.

EDUCATION AND TRAINING

Ultimately labels like *humanistic* and *traditional* tell little either substantive or qualitative about teacher activities. They do not much help our efforts to understand and improve school practices. Exceedingly important, however, is the individual and programmatic meaning used for the term *education* or, to put it differently, the sense of the ideal of becoming an educated person that is held by a teacher and embedded in any program, curriculum, school system, and nation. A grasp of one's own and others' ideals of the educated person is essential to developing a critical perspective on education because that notion, whether articulated or not, informs all practice. It follows that without a conscious sense of an ideal of becoming educated, teaching cannot be understood as an emancipatory activity undertaken with will and clear intention.

The term *education* is difficult to define, but it is important to do so for from definitions come criteria that enable analysis of programs and practices. We will provide a definition and evaluate EBCE according to the standards that define education and differentiate it from processes of training. For EBCE, like any other program, the question is, What traits, qualities, virtues, and characteristics should the educated person have?

To use the term *education* in the sense of the ideal of an educated person means that some kinds of processes must necessarily be employed in trying to achieve the ideal. For the most part, both the means used and the ends sought are thought to be good in a moral sense; that is, we look upon being educated as a desirable thing to happen to a person. We are thus suggesting that there are criteria available for judging whether a person has been well educated or not, and therefore that standards exist for judging the educationally desirable results of school practices. Let us consider the general features of what is involved in becoming educated in order to distinguish an educated person from one who is not. The ensuing discussion of the criteria of education is based on and much indebted to R.S. Peters. Following Peters, we identify three standards or criteria for judging whether the schooling processes a person experiences add up to her becoming educated. These criteria are (1) the enhancement of character and intellect, (2) broadness of knowledge and grasp, and (3) a sense of commitment.[3]

The first criterion, enhancement of character and intellect, suggests that specific personal traits considered universally desirable and beneficial should be developed by the educational process. By contrast then, any schooling activities that teach hate, greed, or blind obedience to authority or thwart the nourishing of logical and question-raising capacities—our practical and emancipatory needs in our terms — are not educative processes. They may train people very well indeed, as history too sharply shows, but they do not promote the education of a person because they do not enhance character and intellect. EBCE does not try to implant pernicious doctrines — indeed the opposite is intended — but the ideals of character and intellect it promotes seem too narrowly constrained by the marketplace. Our analysis disclosed, for example, that normative issues about the placements were seldom raised in the students' projects or with the learning coordinators whereas enthusiasm, contractual responsibility, and persistence were prominent aims of these experiences. Although there is nothing wrong with these attributes, there is also nothing universally desirable about them. They do not unambiguously signify enhancement of character and intellect.

The second criterion, broadness of knowledge and grasp, indicates that the contents learned should cultivate understanding of the interconnections between a wide variety of subjects, events, and experiences. This means that history as a historical grasp of the present ought to become a lively element in one's learning. It suggests that subject matter such as the physical, biological, and social sciences, mathematics, literature, art, music, and philosophy must be well learned if *schooling* is really to foster education. It is of course true that there are plenty of people we would call educated who never went to any school yet show broadness of knowledge and grasp as well as the other criteria. Certainly there are many possible nonformal ways to embrace this standard of broadness; people educate themselves through a variety of means. But schools are precisely the social institutions charged with the task of developing educated persons through formal curricula. Again, our discussions revealed that EBCE seems especially weak in contributing to this second criterion. In particular we saw that what passes for academic credit in the program subverts the values of knowledge, understanding, and grasp that can be gained from study of the traditional curriculum. The too narrow focus on vocations and on accumulating credits for graduation vitiates broadness of knowledge and grasp and thereby frustrates the process of becoming educated.

The third criterion, commitment, the most difficult to describe and assess, is probably the most important of the three. It is likely the one standard that EBCE helps encourage. Commitment, which must touch a person becoming educated, refers to internalizing the standards and educational values one has learned such that they imbue one's outlook, intentions, and activities. Perhaps a simpler way to state this is to say that in becoming educated, one adopts as one's own the standards of excellence inhering in the craft, calling, or processes one has studied. When such craft, calling, or process ideals pervade decisions and reflections, then what has been learned makes an important difference; it counts for something in one's life. Such learning is vital, part and parcel of one's identity. For a teacher this means striving to embody the highest craft ideals in every relevant teaching activity, and the same must hold for the potter, biologist, lab technician, or mechanic. We have all no doubt suffered the consequences of mechanics, technicians, and physicians who never internalized their craft's standards of excellence. Very likely the prime source for learning these standards and thus for learning commitment is the teacher of the various crafts and callings. It is thus possible, even probable, that while training someone in a skill, the good skills teacher will be truly educative because she is excellent in that endeavor. A real educator is herself the criterion of commitment, tacitly teaching by example a model to be emulated. For the high school student facing many possible callings, crafts, and careers, EBCE, by virtue of the range of resources it makes available, may provide rich opportunities for developing a feeling for commitment to standards of excellence, if not the commitment itself. Of course commitment in the sense we have been urging can only be judged over time; nevertheless, at least as far as involvement with their resources goes, EBCE students seem to adopt the criteria of excellence that successful business people embody—hard work, persistence, punctuality, responsibility. In this sense EBCE may be considered educative with regard to commitment although its shortcomings on the other two criteria mean that it is essentially a training program, a long way from helping the young reach the ideal of an educated person.

Chapter 6

Shaping the Democratic Citizen

DEMOCRACY AS PROCEDURE AND ETHIC

For Americans democracy is an often-mentioned but seldom-questioned concept. Its meaning is assumed because we are born into a society that calls itself democratic. For most Americans the term is probably synonymous with a republican form of government; it is something good that means having a procedure for choosing representatives, exercising the vote, and holding a faith in majority rule and in institutionalized checks and balances on the use of power. From this viewpoint democracy is embodied in present institutions and requires only minor and periodic adjustments, such as the 1964 Civil Rights Act, to maintain its virtue. When the concept is so conceived, a citizen has few identifiable responsibilities except for marking a ballot on election day.

But democracy is more than a procedure and a belief in majority rule; it is also a social and ethical ideal rooted in the Enlightenment. In this sense democracy means a set of values to be cultivated and cherished, a desirable way of life. Central to these values is how public knowledge is to be created and used. The positive ideal, to use Habermas's phrase, is "discussion free from domination."[1] That is, the question about how public knowledge is to be created and used is a matter to be settled by free and open discourse among equals.

As an ethic democracy derives from the communication and emancipation interests Habermas finds inhering in reason. The attempt to realize democracy, though fated to fall short in our always less than perfect world, is also condemned to recur continually. The endeavor to create better approximations of democracy is the persistent striving of our emancipatory interest, of reason, to express itself in political institutions and social practices. This infrangible link between democracy and human interest universalizes the struggle for equality and justice in the face of constant denial and suppression of rights. Taken seriously, democracy is subversive precisely because its ideal of public knowledge created through free and open discourse among equals demands continuous justification for the established distribution of power. It will not permit the systematic distortions and repressions that maintaining unwarranted advantage requires.

Although technocratic values, stemming from reason's interest in control, are virtually universal, cultural traditions also honor and try to sustain reason's interest in freedom. As social institutions representing these traditions, public schools must pay lip service at least to this interest. Democracy in particular is a tradition that has enjoyed special status in American educational thought, for the common wisdom says that the survival of our republic depends on the proper education of citizens. In this chapter, through the study of a school district and one high school, we explore how democracy is conceived in a citizenship project, "The Democratic School." Along the way we analyze some of the conflict between democratic and technocratic values and attempt a partial answer to the question "Can democratic values challenge the hegemony of technocratic values in schools?" Finally we discuss how the emotive power of the term *democracy* justifies domination and public deception for administrative and strategic purposes.

SOUTH HIGH AS A DEMOCRATIC SCHOOL

The Salt Lake City School District has for several years given attention to identifying and adopting democratic principles to be used as guides in school governance and as goals for teaching. One school in the district, South High School, is identified as a school in which substantial progress has occurred in making school governance more democratic and in teaching democratic principles to students. During the time of our study, South was participating in a funded democratic school project. Because of these efforts, South High and the Salt Lake City district provide a good setting for studying the meaning and possibilities of democratic citizenship education in public high schools.

South is one of four high schools in the Salt Lake City School District. It is located near the downtown section of the city and has experienced, in a mild form, many of the problems faced by inner city schools throughout the United States. The student body changed over the past several years from a middle- and working-class mixture to a predominantly working-class group. It is now made up of approximately 1,300 students in grades nine through twelve of whom 46 percent are minority — black, Native American, Chicano, and recently, Southeast Asian. The school serves recent immigrants, who now comprise one-sixth of the student body, as a port of entry school. Such schools emphasize learning English and cultural awareness.

Members of the faculty report that only a few years ago conditions at South were such that it was difficult to teach there. Some portions of the campus were felt to be unsafe, especially an area in which unruly groups of students gathered to smoke cigarettes and marijuana. One teacher described this part of the building as having a "blue haze" over it. Vandalism was a serious problem, caused in part by nonstudents who drifted through the school more or less at will.

Conditions at South deteriorated until the faculty joined with the administration to solve some of the most pressing problems. The governance structure of the school was changed to increase the influence of teachers and parents on aspects of school policy. This was part of a district thrust to bring educational practices into greater agreement with the following list of twelve democratic principles that had been adopted as school board policy.

1. Each individual has dignity and worth.
2. A free society requires respect for persons, property, and principles.
3. Each individual has a right to learn and the freedom to achieve.
4. Each individual, regardless of race, creed, color, sex, ethnic background or economic status, has equal opportunity.
5. Each individual has the right to personal liberties.
6. Each individual is responsible for his/her own actions.
7. Each individual has a responsibility to the group as well as to the total society.
8. Democratic governments govern by majority vote.
9. Democratic societies are based on law.

10. Problems are solved through reason and orderly processes.
11. An individual should be tolerant of other religious beliefs and should have freedom to exercise his/her own.
12. Each individual has the right to work, to pursue an occupation and to gain satisfaction from personal efforts.[2]

These twelve statements are at once principles to be taught to students and guides for how schools should operate. The active involvement of teachers in school governance in fact seemed to help better conditions at South. Those we interviewed reported that attendance improved, vandalism was dramatically reduced, student failure rates declined, and teacher morale was on the upswing.

This change in the conditions at South was mentioned as a major reason for its selection to participate in a three-year democratic school project funded by the Danforth Foundation. The purpose of the project was, as South's principal told us, to "put the governance of the school, the governance of the classroom, and the way teachers work with youngsters in congruence with those twelve democratic principles." The first year of the project was devoted to planning, educating the faculty and getting them involved in identifying problems, and forming task forces to work on problems. The second year emphasized developing curricula and strategies for teaching the twelve principles. In the third year of the grant, special attention will be on communicating to other schools what has been learned at South. The project is directed by two teachers from South's faculty who work closely with the principal and outside consultants.

The foregoing details provide a context for later discussion and also show that this high school and school district, unlike many others, have gone a long way beyond merely stating and then ignoring some vague goals about educating democratic citizens. Rather our study is of a place making considerable effort to teach and operate by a set of ideals it has developed and called democratic.

We began our study in the spring of the first year of the project by conducting interviews with the three persons in charge of the program, the principal and the two teacher-directors. The following year we made more visits to the school and again interviewed these persons and additional teachers charged with responsibilities such as student government and the PTA. We also read the documents and reports on the program's development and progress. We did not interview a great many teachers nor did we visit classrooms because our intention was to understand the meaning of democracy held by those involved in creating the program.

DEMOCRATIC ORTHODOXY

A school obviously does not become immediately democratic because it participates in a democratic school project or because the school board has mandated that twelve democratic principles will guide what happens. Projects in democracy must begin with the conceptions educators and students hold about how a democratic school differs from any other school. What that meant for the directors of the democratic school project is forcefully suggested by the two examples they gave as major accomplishments of the school's use of democracy: getting and keeping students out of the hallways during class periods and establishing schoolwide consistency in how student absences and tardinesses were treated. As examples of democracy at work, these acts reveal both the possibilities of using democratic processes for producing change and how an institution's legitimate claims eviscerate democracy's potential as an ideal. The two acts can be viewed as hopeful because of the increased participation of the faculty in solving problems interfering with their ability to teach. However, the constraints imposed by a hierarchical institution are also evident in the extent of student exclusion from important school life decisions.

The new hall policy was described in interview this way: "We have what we call a hall policy. We feel that it's improper to have kids in the halls. . . . We recognize when you get into a big school, there's going to be movement. . . . but we require the teacher to write them a little note. . . . If they don't have the note, the teacher [monitor] merely takes the student's name, turns it into our office, and we deal with it." An important element of the policy is that in the process of discussing what could be done about the confusion in the halls, teachers had agreed to give up some of their class preparation time to monitor these areas. The principal could not have required teachers to do this, but as teachers joined with administrators to try to improve the learning climate at South, they agreed to accept the burdens of the solution they felt conditions required. It seems to be this aspect of the development of a hall policy that the principal and the co-directors point to with pride as an illustration of democracy at work. This also seems an important part of the meaning democracy holds for Americans, meaning suggested though not captured by at least three of the twelve democratic principles: (1) "Each individual has a responsibility to the group as well as to the total society"; (2) "Democratic governments govern by majority vote"; and (3) "Problems are solved through reason and orderly process." It is the belief or trust that if people are allowed to determine the rules, they will accept solutions and commit themselves to act in ways that are more than merely self-serving. Given a voice in improving conditions at South High, teachers had confirmed the trust in people that democracy requires. At least that is one way of understanding why a new hall policy was discussed with pride. As one of the co-directors stated, "Teachers are the ones who are setting a lot of the policies whereas before when a policy comes from above, you give lip service to it, you pretend you're doing it, but you never do it. The teachers are trying to improve the school because we've got to live here, this is where we work."

Our enthusiasm for the democratic character of the hall monitoring is tempered by two concerns. First, the policy was made by teachers working with administrators but not with students even though the latter are directly affected by it. Second, large numbers of students in the halls during class time perhaps indicate problems with curriculum and instruction unlikely to be touched by keeping the hallways clear. This approach to problem solution is typical of a technocratic society, wherein problems are defined such that only minor adjustments are required of a system presumed sound. But if the idea and rhetoric of democracy are used to encourage and increase compliance, can this be democracy? We think not. Our concerns were supported by one teacher who reported in an informal interview, "Before they cleaned up the halls there was too little teaching—lots of noise, kids in the halls, and every teacher's door closed—and now there is too little teaching, but obviously the causes are different." Whether conditions are as this teacher reports we cannot say, but he does locate part of the issue. The emancipatory potential of democracy is dissipated if the efforts of those involved focus on "how to" questions about making the institution function more efficiently rather than on using discussion to raise normative questions of substance. However, the hall and attendance policies are used as examples of early accomplishments in the democratic school project and can be excused as beginning points.

The more fundamental concern we have about the hall policy is that the orderly process created to solve the problem emerged in a conference between administrators and teachers without student involvement. In addition neither the policy, the process, nor the procedure established to deal with student offenders was subjected to the vote of the student body, contradicting principle 8. Why was this so? And without discussion leading to a vote, in what sense can the monitoring program be an example of democracy at work? A partial response is again to note that institutions change slowly and it cannot be expected that inconsistencies between school practice and the democratic principles will be removed quickly. While true this explanation does not show why monitoring is given as a preeminent example of democracy at work when the rights of students to be involved in determining policies that affect them are not honored.

It is ironical that the monitoring program's success as an example of school democracy required using the twelve principles to justify excluding student involvement, a disquieting instance of limiting citizen participation in the name of democracy. How this justification was made offers insight into how democracy is conceived. In an interview one of the co-directors urged that some school matters are simply not voted on, though they might be formally discussed by students and teachers, because they are institutionally mandated. Where issues related to mandated behavior arise, we were told, consensus rather than majority rule is the desired approach: "Consensus [in a democracy] is better than majority rule."

The point is deceptively simple: The institutional boundaries of schooling permit only a narrow range of issues to be the subject of full and open discussion and the vote. Were other issues allowed, the institutional character of schooling would come under question: "You can only talk about democratic schools so much before students want to tax the system— test it." This testing must be contained. When such issues do arise, as they must given anything approximating open discussion, a consensus favorable to the institution needs to be produced. Consensus presumably comes through discussion but appears in fact to be more a matter of a general and unreflective acceptance of the institutional constraints of schooling. This point is critical for understanding the meaning of "reason" within principle 10. For instance, there is little apparent recognition of tension existing between democratic and institutional values though there is fear that democracy, incorrectly conceived, will lead to anarchy. Where this acceptance is in place, discussion will generally lead to institutionally desired outcomes because no other outcomes are seen as reasonable. The basic assumption seems to be that those who hold higher status positions in the institution also have a better understanding of what those below them require; thus any disagreement students might have with the actions of teachers and administrators would of necessity be unreasonable and self-serving, an attempt to acquire unfair advantage.

The acceptance of institutional priorities, a manifestation of technocratic-mindedness, results in the domination of system-maintenance problems (problems with the potential to disrupt the system and perhaps throw it into question) to the *partial* exclusion of normative questions. That is, what is taken as reasonable is bounded by the nature of the institution. This helps to explain why South began work on procedures, not on more substantive issues. The taken-for-granted status of institutional values is evident in one co-director's assertion that while students did not vote on the hall policy, "it would have passed anyway because most students attend classes." The point, however, is that consensus was assumed and not produced through discussion and debate though, as the co-director pointed out, it would have passed anyway. The students did not vote because in fact they could not have rejected the policy; this was not an option even had they wished it. Further, voting on whether or not students should be allowed in the hallways was not reasonable.

Additional light is shed upon the program's operational definition of democracy when we consider another example given of democracy at work: the attendance policy, developed following receipt of the grant. This example confirms what we have thus far argued and offers opportunity for further analysis. Like noisy hallways, the lack of an adequate policy to govern attendance and deal with offending students was identified as a concern shared by teachers and administrators and was thus a candidate for "democratic process." Prior to the new policy's implementation, a teacher might have given a student with several tardies and absences a passing grade while another teacher failed a second student with an identical record. Or one teacher who was careless in marking his roll might have given a passing grade to a student who was failed by a teacher who kept more accurate records. One result of this situation was that students could "play one teacher against the other."

This problem was identified along with several others by the faculty and administration in "little workshops" organized as part of the democratic school project. As a common problem requiring joint action, it became the focus of one of the six task forces composed of faculty and charged with democratizing South High School. We can pose some of the same questions here as we did earlier with monitoring. Specifically, how can such a problem and the policy that was created to deal with it be understood and defended as democratic and in what sense of democracy? Again, one of the co-directors offers a partial answer: "Attendance, although it doesn't sound like a part of the democratic process . . ., is . . . well, it's like in a democracy where one person pays his tax and the other one doesn't. The person who pays his tax really resents the fact that some rich dude has found the loophole. The same thing here. . . . one student is really upset because one teacher allows a lot of loopholes [in attendance] and another teacher doesn't. . . . [It's a matter] of fairness." We do not know if in fact the students were upset about the lack of consistency, but it is worth noting that the interests of the students were used as the grounds for the democratic legitimacy of this problem.

Fairness, in the sense used here, means that each student is to be treated identically, is subjected to the same rules and penalties for misbehavior. It also means that some teachers cannot be trusted to create with students the rules for governing their own classrooms. When a student has accumulated five absences (forty-five minutes of tardy time equals one absence), he is brought before the Attendance Review Committee, composed of three students, three teachers, and an administrator. The offending student presents a case to this committee and may request leniency. If an appeal is accepted, the student can enter negotiations with his teachers to make up for work lost. In this way justice is to be served. If an appeal is denied, then credit is lost.

Fairness, understood as receiving the same treatment, was directly related by the co-directors to principle 9, "Democratic societies are based on law." One commented that "democratic governments are based upon rules . . . that's one thing we're trying to stress to our students. Rules are part of democracy." Without them democracy becomes "anarchy." Hence fairness is a matter of all students being equally subjected to laws, or school rules in this case. Students must attend school and, with respect to the hall policy, keep out of the hallways without valid reason or else receive punishment for "taxing the system." If students do not go along with these requirements, then the survival of the institution is threatened. But much hinges on who creates these rules or laws, and how they are created and enforced. As with the hall policy, attendance is prescribed and is therefore not open to full debate. Yet unlike the hall policy, the attendance policy was voted upon by the students. Why? What is the difference?

As noted, the hall policy was taken to be a matter for consensus. Students were not to be in the halls without written reason, without adult consent. The attendance policy, however, offered more room for negotiation. Students could not "reasonably" urge a policy allowing nonattendance with credit (though many students were off campus in approved programs for which credit was received), but they could argue for and vote upon either a more or less lenient policy, say six as opposed to five absences without automatic credit loss. The policy, including the recommended procedures to deal with offending parties, was opened to debate and vote. In some instances discussion was spirited. But one wonders if the outcome, given the acceptance of institutional values, was ever in doubt. Further, it is likely that as indicated in interviews, for most students, particularly the better ones, attendance is a nonissue. It is only an issue for the recalcitrant and intermittently attending minority.

Voting, in this instance, is particularly important to the school because the dissenting minority is held, under the democratic principles, as duty bound to uphold the decisions of the majority (principle 8). If dissenters do not like the rules, they are under obligation to help change them. Students who run afoul of the attendance policy have presumably broken a law that was accepted as legitimate. Hence (principles 6 and 7) the dictates of fair play and justice demand punishment. Among those who are to establish punishment and to review appeals are three peers who sit on the Attendance Review Committee, and though in the minority on the committee, add to the legitimacy of decisions by their presence and participation.

Fairness is ensured throughout the program by emphasizing and standardizing procedure. Whatever problems arise, there are now pre-scribed ways for dealing with them so that ideally all individual problems of a similar kind are treated in like manner. Evident here is a great faith in systems to treat human problems consistently and therefore fairly. As a value fairness is implied throughout the twelve democratic principles and is recognized as essential to the realization of the larger school goal of improving the learning climate. As so often happens, however, the emphasis on procedure, on a procedural conception of fairness, contra-dicts other essential values of democracy. The attendance policy provides an illustration. As with the monitoring program, we must ask who deter-mines what is a reasonable and orderly process for problem solving? We have already noted that this policy was established by the teachers and administrators though it was ratified by the students. Presumably a "demo-cratic process" is to be followed in all problem solving so that the same qualities will characterize faculty, administrator, and student inter-actions.

We will first consider the procedure used to identify the solution to the attendance problem. As noted, a task force was charged with responsi-bility for conceiving an attendance policy. To address this problem it was "insisted that they [members of the task force] go through a problem-solving procedure." The procedure used was a variation of the Delphi Technique, which is a way of producing consensus with minimal discussion, conflict, and dissent. (Again we see the value of consensus.) A list of possible solutions to a problem is circulated among involved parties. Each time the list goes around, preferred solutions are marked and less popular ones are dropped until ideally a single solution emerges. Once the solution is identified, what remains is the technical and sometimes political question of how it is to be implemented most efficiently. The virtue of the technique urged by the principal was that is prevents domination by "the most vocal person." It also, however, lessens the likelihood of conflict among the faculty, which was generally understood as destabilizing: "We've avoided any major catastrophes" with the faculty. Yet the democratic ethic always implies conflict among opinions and beliefs as well as a faith that ultimately common values will emerge. Such conflict can only be circumvented at the expense of the values of democracy. Its suppression, whether intentionally or through presumably benign procedures, results in the reinforcement of the present distribution of power, thus confirming status and hierarchical institutional arrangements. In this instance the "orderly process" selected to produce a policy runs counter to other more fundamental democratic values by constricting discussion and by establishing a limited and technical conception of participation.

The procedure that emerged from the attendance policy for dealing with offending students also appears in some respects to run counter to fundamental democratic principles. In the name of fairness, this procedure is inserted between the teacher and student; it mediates their relationship by establishing the basis upon which communication can and will take place. A few teachers appeared to be highly dissatisfied with this practice, in part because they saw it as an unwarranted incursion into their professional activities. As one teacher put it, "Ultimately I should decide how well [the students] have done in my class." But there is more at stake here. This teacher desired to be trusted to do what was in the best interest of his students. Hence this is not simply a matter of trespass on a few teachers' turfs; it is a question of trust, without which democracy cannot become vital.

The hall and attendance policies reveal something more concrete about how the school and district conceive of democracy beyond the rather nebulous but appealing statement of principles. First, their conception is based upon a distrustful view of human nature. That is, where institutional boundaries might be threatened or where the smooth operation of the school may be potentially disrupted, discussion appears to be constrained and outcomes assured. Thus the value of consensus. But as noted, this is an artificial consensus. It is only a projection of an unreflective acceptance of institutional values rather than a product of free and open discourse. Second, the problems that are to be the focus of democratic process appear primarily to be those having to do with maintaining the system, though fortunately there are some important exceptions, which will be discussed shortly. These problems have come to be seen as concerns for all school participants. Third, the emphasis on procedure appears in some respects to have replaced the substantive discussion so necessary for honoring the claims of justice. The possibility of value conflict is thereby reduced. Such conflict is thought of as system threatening, as leading to anarchy. The choice is between order and chaos, and the tendencies of democracy to disorder must be repressed. Fourth, participation of students is circumscribed and comes as a privilege rather than a right resting in the sovereignty of the people.

These beliefs or values can only be democratic in a peculiar sense, as an orthodoxy essentially consistent with institutional values where ends are known in advance. In spite of some claims to the contrary, this appears to be the case. The challenge for the leaders of the program is to make certain this orthodoxy "trickles down" and is accepted by the faculty. The leaders are grateful they "h.. e time to work with the faculty. Whatever their attitudes were in September and October, we have had plenty of time to change them, and to work with them." The students will in turn learn democracy from their teachers: "People learn democratic behavior from people who behave democratically." They will also learn these values through "indoctrination," which "is legitimate as long as students are made aware of [it]." Some teachers have found this orthodoxy troubling. The principal reports, for instance, that early in the program some teachers raised quite a fuss in one faculty meeting. "Boy, they were mad. They were telling us that we knew what the answer was going to be and we were just leading them on and why didn't we tell them. . . . We had to do our very best to convince them that that was not the case." This effort was only somewhat successful; for some teachers democracy remains a desirable and highly problematic ideal rather than an orthodoxy to be indoctrinated.

ORTHODOXY AS POLICY

As an orthodoxy based upon twelve true principles, democracy is viewed as analogous in many respects to those content areas grounded in science and based upon laws of nature. It is assumed democracy can and ought to be taught and tested like any other content or skill area; the proof of learning is in the behavioral changes evidenced by students such as, for instance, less vandalism and better, more consistent attendance. For efficiency reasons democracy, so understood, should be directly inculcated in the young.

Where this view obtains at the district level, it is difficult, given the hierarchical structure of American schooling, to imagine a busy school faculty opting for a different, perhaps even opposing conception. Establishing the legitimacy of an opposing view would indeed be a formidable though perhaps not impossible task. But this was apparently not necessary at South High School for two reasons: The teachers generally accepted district policies, and there was little to take offense at, perhaps in part because the teachers' own senses of democracy were vague. From an orthodox perspective, teachers who lack proper understanding of democracy are much like students and in need of instruction in the principles, the true conception of democracy. We suspect this view of democracy is widely held and captures the conventional belief about what the schools ought to be doing about values education. A brief description of the district's efforts to identify and then develop ways of teaching and evaluating democratic values will shed further light on the origins of the orthodoxy and, most importantly, upon its claims to truth.

The twelve principles were developed "after substantial study (including an extensive review of the literature and examination of our own situation) and after a national conference on citizenship education was held in Salt Lake City." It was concluded that "current ethical systems are based on pluralism, relativism, and the principle that ends justify means." This unhappy state of affairs necessitated the "return to individual ethics based on the philosophical writings of Immanuel Kant and the principles written into our national documents."[3] Though it is unclear precisely what is meant here, it is assumed that there are moral universals that possess lawlike characteristics upon which the health of the nation and the happiness of the individual rest. For the good of society, the individual must internalize these principles or, stated differently, come to willingly behave in accordance with moral law.* These laws or principles are built into our national ethos and can be culled directly from our "national documents." Failure to uphold the principles is, by inference, responsible for many of our national ills.

---

*Some of the twelve principles are normative and have an "ought" quality to them while others appear to be descriptive. Yet in practice all of them are taken as normative.

Defined in terms of rules and attitudes, democracy can be taught like other content areas and tested. This belief is suggested in a descriptive statement of what has thus far been accomplished in the Salt Lake City School District. The district

1. Passed a Board of Education policy requiring competence in ethics and moral behavior prior to graduation from high school.
2. Based its ethics education program on individual ethics.
3. Established 12 statements as ethical universals to be taught. These universals have been extracted from our national documents.
4. Required that each teacher develop a learning unit based on these principles.
5. Provided inservice training for teachers and administrators.
6. Appointed a teacher leader in the area of ethics education.
7. Gave financial support to ethics education programs established in various schools.
8. Published teaching units in ethics education for teacher use.
9. Developed instruments to evaluate ethics education in the district.[4]

The call upon a national ethos and national documents for support of the program has obvious polemic value, but it does not help us to understand what the principles are in fact supposed to mean. Which ethos and which national documents underpin the orthodox view? One need only compare the Declaration of Independence with the Constitution to be thrown into a quandary; which document holds the correct interpretation of democracy? Can both be read in such a way as to suggest the same conception of democracy? The former defends the right of revolution and recognizes the inevitability of conflict while the latter establishes checks and balances to prevent revolutionary action and contain conflict. It is apparent therefore that only a particular reading of these documents and a particular understanding of our national ethos allows establishment of a democratic orthodoxy, in this case an institutionally specific view of democracy. Are other interpretations uninformed or simply wrongheaded? Whence then comes the truth status of the orthodoxy? And are the principles to be unquestioned?

Ultimately the status of these principles as truth rests upon an assertion by those at the top of the hierarchy that there are moral universals and that the twelve principles are of this class. Further, the principles work, that is, they are useful in making an institution run more smoothly and efficiently. The latter statement suggests that democracy's utility is that it makes for a better life and a better life is produced through better operating institutions, not through making the grounds upon which these institutions rest problematic. The real test of democracy is that "we have seen a marked improvement in student behavior" and, one might add, through in-service training, in teacher behavior.

While it might be a bit too harsh a judgment, it appears that the talk about democracy in the Salt Lake City schools is used to legitimate what exists. The truth of the principles is found primarily in how well they serve established institutional ends. From this perspective the twelve principles are much like advertising slogans used to sell a product, a prescribed way of living within an institution that is undemocratic.

GROUNDS FOR HOPE

Given the institutional character of schooling and the predominance of technocratic-mindedness, it is little wonder that the operational definition of democracy guiding South High School would be permeated with technical values. In this view the good citizen within an institution is the organization man who works hard, accepts the company's priorities, and defends its honor. The result is that democratic values are disfigured and their emancipatory potential blunted but not lost.

In chapter 2 we listed several prominent assumptions of technocratic-mindedness related to schooling. We noted that underlying these assumptions is a pervasive valuing of the control believed necessary to the attainment of a production conception of efficiency within institutions. Standardization of human experience, avoidance of conflict as destabilizing, elevation of systems and procedures over human judgment, constriction of the arena of professional decision making to means, reduction of learning to proper behavior, separation and specialization of functions, and accountability to externally established goals are in varying degrees all present and desired within South High School, as we have demonstrated. Under these conditions it is reasonable to ask if there is any purpose whatsoever in trying to democratize a high school. The answer is "yes" from two perspectives: one grounded in our work interest and the value of control, the other in our emancipatory interest.

Given the intention of indoctrinating values, we asked one of the leaders of the project why they chose to speak of democratic rather than moral education. The answer we received was somewhat surprising. At least part of the reason "democracy" was selected was because they "didn't want to spend all of [their] time defending morality and ethics." The point was that to speak of morality implies that religious and sexual values are being taught that would likely lead to public expressions of concern and conflict, as it has in schools throughout the United States. In contrast the democratic tradition is understood as offering a set of values that are widely accepted, relatively innocuous, and seldom thought about: "That's why we have those principles . . . no one is going to disagree with them." Indoctrination of values can then be practiced with relative impunity, for few persons would stop to ask questions about the meaning of democracy; its taken-for-granted goodness makes questioning unnecessary. However, the values indoctrinated represent a democratic orthodoxy consistent with current institutional priorities. Its usefulness is in helping achieve a particular moral and ethical unity with minimal tension, controversy, or conflict.

It is true, on the face of it, that the twelve democratic principles offer little reason for disagreement. Few Americans would, for instance, argue against principle 1, "Each individual has dignity and worth," or principle 3, "Each individual has a right to learn and the freedom to achieve." But what do these statements mean? What does it mean, for example, to expel a student while honoring his dignity and worth? It is at this point where disagreement is likely to occur and where values become evident. A statement made by one of the co-directors illustrates the difficulty: "Every human being has — deserves — the dignity of being treated as a human being no matter what sort of creep he may act like or prove himself to be. He still deserves that respect as a human being. . . . That doesn't mean he won't be kicked out of school, or that he won't fail. But it means that he won't be treated as a beast while he's being kicked out of school or failing." Similarly, what does it mean to have the "freedom to achieve"? How is freedom understood? Is it a gift, a right, a condition, an accomplishment? Does it have limits? If so, who or what imposes them? And what counts as an infringement on an individual's freedom? Does grading or attendance qualify? Apparently the virtue of the twelve principles is that they ring true and prevent careful consideration of what is being taught.

Democracy has of course long been used to mask efforts aimed at maintaining the favored positions of individuals and groups; often it has been taken as identical with current institutional structures and priorities since we live in a society that calls itself democratic. As a form of government in competition with other governments, democracy has been a slogan used to justify a wide range of questionable actions from invasions of other nations to blacklisting. One reason such actions are undertaken is to preserve and protect established institutions. But as an ethic, democracy is likely threatening to these very institutions. This potential is evident, for example, where democracy serves as a rallying cry for the oppressed. Appropriating democracy to justify institutional priorities and to facilitate control is risky, for it is a concept that speaks to our emancipatory interest.

The governmental and ethical baggage that democracy brings with it is intermixed in the twelve principles. Hence in addition to talk about law, "democratic process," voting, and procedure, there is talk about equality, rights, respect, and fairness. Talk about respect has produced some much desired results. For instance teachers and students are confronting racism in the school. One co-director reported the following episode:

> A couple of days ago a student in class was making fun of a racial minority. So we immediately — first of all, I stopped it. And then I asked him — he was making fun of black speech. So rather than let it go and say, "No, you can't say that," I said, "Okay, where did the blacks come from?" And they said, "The South." And I said, "Well, how do blacks speak then?" And he said, "Well, like Southerners." Then a girl says, "Yeah, I have a neighbor who came from England and he's lived in our country thirty years and guess what, he still speaks like, he speaks like an Englishman." I say, "Okay, let's go take this one step further. Do you think Utahns have any speech patterns peculiar to this area?" Right away, all of a sudden, we began . . . talking about it. . . . The kid, afterwards said, "You know, I was joking around." I said, "I know you were just joking around but can you see that's the kind of stuff that breeds intolerance?"

While it may be the case that the underlying economic and institutional causes of racism are not being confronted and studied, some of its ugly manifestations are being challenged. This is certainly an important accomplishment that, along with other program changes, has made school a much more pleasant experience.

Previously, we discussed how "fairness" appears to be primarily a matter of same treatment of students, a bureaucratic rendering of the idea. By this we mean established rules and procedures dictate how all individual cases are to be handled. However, when summoned by the sweet call of justice, that narrow sense of fairness must be transcended. "Fairness" as justice signifies different treatment of individuals, especially those least favored, and demands having good reasons at hand for bending rules or suspending procedures. This tension between the uniform application of rules and the claims of justice is ever present and further heightened by the fact that facilitating student development sometimes requires breaching procedures.

Fairness, in this larger sense, has required planning a teacher advocate system whereby a student who is threatened with explusion, say, for fighting, may be represented by a teacher he likes and respects. In principle this teacher, charged with the responsibility of presenting the student's side of the story, would be placed in opposition to the institution. It is not yet clear how teacher advocates will operate, but there would appear to be a strong likelihood that serious normative questions will be raised. We will have to wait and see what emerges. Unfortunately there is a danger that the teacher advocate will become primarily a means for making the student feel better about being expelled rather than a means for protecting his rights.

Further, in this larger sense, talking about fairness, rights, and equality brought about student participation on a variety of formerly exclusive school committees. While these committees are generally charged with maintenance responsibilities, they occasionally address policy-related issues. For instance, three students sit on the Attendance Review Committee. On this committee they hear student cases and are therefore confronted with issues bearing on the quality of school life and on justice and fair play. They must weigh institutional requirements against their peers' interests.

Where talk about respect for persons, fairness, equality, and rights becomes common and constant, as it is in South High School, there is the likelihood that eventually contrary questions—learned in school through literature, the movies, and elsewhere—will be raised about institutional practices. Currently most of the questions addressed are about individual practices and priorities that are incongruent with school expectations. While these questions may not alter schooling, they can and do alter the way we understand human life and the institutions designed to serve it. It is here that we find hope, for such questions are persistent and have emancipatory potential.

Chapter 7

Education
for Emancipation

Technocratic-mindedness is, as we have demonstrated, a pervasive and powerful influence on American schooling. It is institutionalized and interwoven into the way we speak and think about the aims and means of education. It informs our standards of teaching excellence and thus our teacher preparation programs; it establishes the boundaries within which legitimacy must be argued; it narrowly defines what is understood as educationally reasonable; and, crucially, it discourages trust in human judgment while promoting an uncritical faith in the efficacy of systems for handling all our situations, moral-political as well as technical.

The power of technocratic-mindedness stems from its being a pre-understanding, a taken-for-granted orientation, an indisputably natural way of comprehending and dealing with life. In the realm of education, this means teachers and administrators share technocratic values about institutional commitments, about processes, and about their respective interests. Thus they may lose the enlightenment that can arise from the vital tension of differing priorities. But there are other human interests that though often ignored still persist, such as our interest in freedom. Education can be emancipatory when it emphasizes communicative interaction and the force of the better idea in deciding the truth of things. Our study shows the tyrannous hold that the need for control has secured over schooling. In this concluding chapter, we will explore the possibility of challenging that tyranny.

Throughout our interviews and observations, we noted that some teachers raised questions that could make technical values problematic.

But the potential for questioning often withers because teachers fail to understand its implications, look for technical solutions to problems, or fall back on blaming themselves or students for difficulties. For instance, like many of her colleagues, one of the GEMS teachers interviewed complained about the pretests and posttests. Her concern was that the same items appeared on both tests and that after taking one and failing it a few times, even a slow student would memorize the proper answers and pass. She wondered how passing in this way could possibly be taken as evidence of learning. The solution, technical in nature, was to write her own exams and only use program posttests at the end of the year in order to make certain that she got "the records onto the computer." Action of this kind is not resistance to institutional or ideological constraints, but it does contain possibility for change; it shows that teachers do not just passively accept, but that they care about their work and are willing to subvert the system, at least in small ways, to make teaching more sensible. Such actions may be misguided, treating symptoms rather than underlying causes. However, even the recognition of symptoms suggests critical thinking and may lead to questioning basic institutional structures. What is absent is a community within which such questions can be asked. Teachers are isolated from one another by the clerking and management tasks they must increasingly take on. And isolation, of course, inhibits dialogue — communicative interaction — with its emancipatory promise. The structure of work, in other words, tends to buttress the status quo by holding in check the opportunities for teachers to get together to discuss how and why their "oughts" about educational means and aims are frustrated.

The learning coordinators of EBCE raised numerous questions about the worth of the regular school program. They saw their work as a challenge to the system they were nevertheless compelled to serve. Their situation prompted a comment that teaching is a "schizophrenic thing." They denounced the regular school program because it failed to meet students' vocational needs and because schooling seemed so dehumanizing to them. However, their belief that a student's survival depended on his getting a job contained their criticism of the regular program. Thus in spite of serious dissatisfaction with schooling and apparent resistance to system demands by both its teachers and students, EBCE reinforced technical values, perhaps to a greater degree than in the standard school program. Nevertheless, given this lack of satisfaction, the relative freedom enjoyed by the learning coordinators, and their obvious intelligence, there is a possibility that other measures of educational values might be created, perhaps ones founded on a critical understanding of the workplace. But first the learning coordinators must begin to doubt their beliefs about the place of job training in education.

Some teachers we spoke with raised normative questions, specifically about the meaning of education and about the quality of life lived in schools, but they did not quite know what to do with their questions. These teachers were generally isolated; they struggled alone in the attempt to keep intellectually, personally, and professionally alive while at work. Often they made small spaces within the curriculum to do activities and to study topics they prized. A high school English teacher we interviewed seems representative of this group. Like some of the teachers whose ideas were discussed in chapter 2, she complained about the testing in GEMS though she accepted it as inevitable. But unlike many of those involved in GEMS, she was not particularly concerned about the lack of quality test items or about the frequency of testing per se. Rather she did not like what was happening to her; she could remember a better time: "Before we had this [program] I think I was much more daring in the kinds of things that I would try. . . . I never had the feeling that the kids suffered." Nor did she like what was happening to many of the students: "It's deadly. It seems to me it [destroys] any desire to learn. . . . It's more something you've got to get through." She also expressed displeasure with her colleagues' perceptions of educational significance, complaining that many important learnings were squeezed out of the curriculum to be replaced by testable "technical things," and that some of her fellow teachers actively facilitated this trend. For example, she reported that during a meeting to set goals a teacher, referring to a particular outcome, remarked, "Well, I don't know —that's a good goal, but I don't know how we can test it, so let's take it out." That attitude perplexed and troubled our respondent: "Wait a minute," she said, "There's something wrong!"

The mere existence of dissatisfaction offers the possibility of creating a different, more growth-enabling teacher role, for it is a necessary condition of critical-mindedness. Hence this teacher is at a juncture in her development. She may resign herself to her situation and keep busy doing technical tasks like coding materials to objectives by way of suppressing her frustration, yet feel the martyr: "If this is what they want—fine. Give them what they want. I know I'm a better teacher than that, but apparently nobody cares." Or she might outwardly accept conditions as they are but try to make things more tolerable by doing only a minimal amount of busywork while producing opportunities to talk with her students about important matters. In addition she might begin reaching out to others in hopes of overcoming her isolation.

The desire to share burdens, to "bitch," is one likely beginning point for overcoming isolation and for starting to make explicit the whys of dissatisfaction. Once the frustrated reaction of placing blame on students, on apparently less competent teachers, or on administrators has worn thin, the potentiality for critical understanding arises. Such understanding has two purposes: It helps teachers comprehend what is, what has been, and why, both institutionally and professionally, and it discloses the desirable and the possible for the situation at hand. Dissatisfaction implies an unrealized sense of the desirable respecting teaching and learning. And the possible can only be determined in the light of the first purpose, comprehension. In this process institutional constraints on role definition and internalized ideological barriers can be confronted, thus resistance begins.

Throughout the country there are signs of increasingly stronger and more persistent dissatisfaction leading to resistance to technocratic resolutions of educational problems. In some places teachers are collectively striving to develop a critical grasp of their discontent. The work of the Boston Women's Teachers' Group is one illustration of this effort.* A desire to gripe and the need for sympathetic ears motivated a small group of Boston teachers to begin meeting weekly in 1976. In varying degrees they were unhappy with teaching. Some faced losing their jobs as budgets were trimmed. Others doubted their ability and contemplated quitting before being "Riffed" (Reduction in Force). Eventually the need to gripe was overshadowed by the desire to understand. As they studied their situations together, the Boston teachers realized that schools are not isolated institutions. They began to see their "work against the larger fabric of economics . . . and history." In reading "theoretical articles about schools, about political economy, or about women as workers," they found their own teaching experiences "illuminated." Gradually they saw their experiences and feelings as more common than they had imagined although they continued to feel "isolated."[1] Something had to be done:

> We knew the topics we were discussing were important, at least to us.
> We also knew that our group was homogeneous in age, race, socio-

---

*We wish to thank Sara Freedman and other members of the Boston Women's Teachers' Group for their kindness in sharing material and ideas. They can be contacted by writing to P.O. Box 169, West Somerville, Massachusetts, 02144.

economic status, and general teaching philosophy. We were not at all sure that our reactions and experiences would parallel other teachers' perceptions whose personal histories were very different from our own.

It became clearer that without an understanding of how teaching had affected many teachers, as well as ourselves, we would be caught in an ever more isolating position. We could find no tools, no framework from educational literature, that would analyze how schools worked and how they had prevented us from reaching out to teachers who taught down the hall or behind the folding partition door. We began to recognize that part of the problem for our continued isolation rested in the model we were using for investigating and improving our own school experiences as teachers. This model, based on a number of influential books written in the late '60's, emphasized the individual contribution by caring teachers whose dedication could significantly alter and improve schools. These books had inspired us as we entered teaching and provided a standard by which we had been judging ourselves and our fellow teachers. Nothing in these books mentioned the powerful influence of the structure of schools on the relationship between the teacher and the child, principal, parent, or specialist.

Several years later, the publication of many articles on teacher burnout reinforced this essentially individualistic point of view. Thus, the teacher literature that we read—the books that had influenced our decisions to enter the profession, and the articles suggesting that we leave—refrained from investigating the areas we had felt to be most painful in our teaching—our growing sense of isolation and alienation from all with whom we came into daily contact: our students, their parents, our fellow teachers, and administrators.

The publication of the articles on teacher burnout coincided with our realization that the teacher support group more frequently clarified our frustrations than it provided resource for alleviating them. We would speak, often with cynicism or bewilderment, of the teacher at the other end of the corridor; but talking to her, learning the background for her action and beliefs, had been considered fruitless. . . . In order to understand how teaching was affecting us and why, we had to know how and why it had affected others. [2]

The research interest of the group emerged slowly in response to specific questions and concerns and in direct contrast to the individualism evident in teacher burnout literature. It was hoped that through research "the isolation of teaching and the paralysis of self-condemnation it often creates" could be broken.[3] Thus was born the Boston Women's Teachers' Group. For two years, with the support of a National Institute of Education grant and other funding, members of the group conducted biweekly interviews, many of which were more dialogical than question-answer, with a selected number of teachers. The general question posed was "How has the structure of the public school and the experience of teaching affected you?" Though the focus was primarily on "structural barriers" to teacher growth and quality of life, other questions and issues that arose along the way were explored, for the aim was critical insight.

Throughout the interviews, dissatisfaction, tension, disillusionment, confusion, and feelings of isolation were pronounced themes. Teachers answered questions "frankly because the thrust of the project corresponded to a felt need of their own, that once articulated, was acknowledged as a gnawing question and the source of unresolved tensions." The process of naming these tensions was often a slow and difficult one. But once named the "roots of the situation" were explored personally, institutionally, and historically, and "possibilities for flexibility" were uncovered.[4]

The Boston Women's Teachers' Group exemplifies what is possible when teachers are unwilling to repudiate their educational ideals or continue to live with the irrational. Rather than individually resigning themselves to their situations, they united and discovered the common threads that bind them together as teachers. Through writing, workshops, talking, and study, they continue to reach out to others in the hope, however slim, of making a difference. Their project is an exciting illustration of developing critical-mindedness. And so, toiling at the roots of their discontent, they present a different vision of teaching's possibilities.

Our own work has much in common with that of the Boston group. It began with dissatisfaction, a strong desire to overcome professional isolation, and a need to understand. As a result of researching and writing, we are more sensitive than ever to the difficulty of effecting institutional change yet more hopeful than before that teachers may come to question the limitations that confront them. We have met and interacted with a number who are trying in various ways to do something about their discontent. They are committed individuals who intend to stay in teaching. A few have come to us for seminars, some we have contacted for talk, and others have developed their own support systems. As these persons meet and interact, they raise normative questions that cast light upon institutional constraints and ideological priorities, those reflections of technocratic-mindedness.

It is our hope that *Human Interests in the Curriculum* will further this process in some small way. That is, we hope it might encourage the critical study of education by all who find something amiss with the current aims and means of schooling or who find the popular criticism of teachers misguided. Perhaps the expectation that critical study will lead to resistance and to institutional change is farfetched; however, as an expression of our communication and emancipation interests, the doing is reward enough. And surely this is reason for hope.

Notes
Selected Bibliography
Index

Notes

CHAPTER 1.   MINDS, SCHOOLING, AND CRITIQUE

1. Michael Polanyi, *The Study of Man* (Chicago: University of Chicago Press, 1958).
2. Don Ihde, "A Phenomenology of Man-Machine Relations," in *Work, Technology and Education*, ed. Walter Feinberg and Henry Rosemont, Jr. (Urbana, Ill.: University of Illinois Press, 1975), p. 190.
3. Paul Willis discusses this apparent contradiction in the lives of working-class English schoolboys in *Learning to Labor: How Working Class Kids Get Working Class Jobs* (New York: Columbia University Press, 1981).
4. See Jurgen Habermas, *Knowledge and Human Interests* (Boston: Beacon Press, 1971), pp. 301–17.
5. The first phrase was stated by Edward L. Thorndike in 1917 to which William McCall added the second in 1922. See William A. McCall, *How to Measure in Education* (New York: Macmillan, 1922), pp. 3–4.
6. Plato, *Apology*, in *The Collected Dialogues of Plato*, ed. Edith Hamilton and Huntington Cairns (Princeton, N.J.: Princeton University Press, 1969), p. 23.

CHAPTER 2.   THE RATIONAL CURRICULUM:
TEACHERS AND ALIENATION

1. Gilbert M. Stevenson and C. Devon Sanderson, "Forward to Basics," mimeographed (Sandy, Utah: Jordan School District, n.d.), p. 1.
2. Ibid.
3. GEMS Science Goal Unit No. 208-101, "In the Beginning," mimeographed (Sandy, Utah: Jordan School District, n.d.), unpaginated.
4. Ibid.
5. Ibid.

6. Ibid.

7. Robert C. Tucker (ed.), *The Marx-Engels Reader,* 2nd edition (New York: W. W. Norton, 1978), p. 74.

CHAPTER 3.   LEARNING TO LABOR

1. Herbert J. Klausmeier, "Individually Guided Education: 1966–1980," *Journal of Teacher Education* 27 (Fall 1976): 199.

2. Paulo Freire, *Pedagogy of the Oppressed* (New York: Herder and Herder, 1968).

3. Michael Polanyi, *Personal Knowledge* (Chicago: University of Chicago Press, 1962).

4. Klausmeier, "Individually Guided Education," p. 200.

5. Ibid.

6. Ibid.

7. Ibid., p. 201.

8. Herbert J. Klausmeier, "Instructional Programming for the Individual Student," in *Individually Guided Elementary Education: Concepts and Practices,* ed. Herbert J. Klausmeier, Richard A. Rossmiller, and Mary Saily (New York: Academic Press, 1977), p. 60.

9. Herbert J. Klausmeier, "Origin and Overview of IGE," in ibid., p. 17.

10. Klausmeier, "Instructional Programming for the Individual Student," p. 70.

11. Ibid.

12. Ibid.

13. Herbert J. Klausmeier, James M. Lipham, and Richard A. Rossmiller, "Continuing Research and Development," in *Individually Guided Elementary Education,* ed. Klausmeier et al., p. 318.

CHAPTER 4.   ART AND THE TECHNOCRATIC IMPERATIVE

1. Ivan E. Cornia, Charles B. Stubbs, and Nathan B. Winters, *Art Is Elementary: Teaching Visual Thinking Through Art Concepts* (Provo, Utah: Brigham Young University Press, 1978), p. 5.

2. Ibid., p. 3.

3. Ibid., p. 5.

4. Ibid., p. 4.

5. Ibid.

6. Ibid., p. 7.

7. Ibid., p. 2.

8. U.S. Department of Education, National Diffusion Network Division, *Educational Programs That Work*, eighth edition (San Francisco: Far West Laboratory for Educational Research and Development, 1981).

9. Wei Li Fang, "The Joint Dissemination Review Panel: Can Approved Submittals Be Distinguished from Rejected Ones on the Basis of Presented Evidence Related to Cognitive Objectives?," mimeographed (Charlottesville, Va.: University of Virginia, n.d.), pp. 36–37.

10. U.S. Department of Education, *JDRP: Joint Dissemination Review Panel*, pamphlet (Washington, D.C.: n.d.).

11. Cornia et al., *Art Is Elementary*, p. 5.

12. Utah State Board of Educaton, *Art Inventory: Test C*, mimeographed (Salt Lake City: Board of Education, 1981), p. 7.

13. Cornia et al., *Art Is Elementary*, p. 7.

14. Ibid., p. 1.

15. Ibid., p. 57.

16. Ibid., p. 366.

CHAPTER 5.   CAREERS AND CONSCIOUSNESS: ALTERNATIVE EDUCATION IN SECONDARY SCHOOLS

1. The Far West Laboratory for Educational Research and Development, *EBCE: The Far West Model, A Program Overview* (San Francisco: Far West Laboratory, n.d.), p. 7.

2. Ibid., p. 7.

3. R.S. Peters, *Ethics and Education* (Glenview, Ill.: Scott, Foresman, 1967), pp. 1–20.

CHAPTER 6.   SHAPING THE DEMOCRATIC CITIZEN

1. Jurgen Habermas, *Toward a Rational Society* (Boston: Beacon Press, 1968).

2. Donald Thomas and Margaret Richards, "Ethics Education Is Possible!" *Phi Delta Kappan* 59 (April 1979): 579–82.

3. Thomas and Richards, "Ethics Education," p. 579.

4. Ibid., pp. 579–80.

CHAPTER 7.   EDUCATION FOR EMANCIPATION

1. Boston Women's Teachers' Group, Sara Freedman, Jane Jackson and Katherine Boles, "The Effects of the Institutional Structure of Schools on

Teachers," Final Report, G-81-0031 (Washington, D.C.: National Institute of Education, September 1, 1982), p. 2.

2. Ibid., pp. 2–3. Quoted by permission.
3. Boston Women's Teachers' Group, "Establishing Teacher-Support Groups and Task Forces to Foster Teacher Initiated Change," xeroxed (West Somerville, Mass.: Boston Women's Teachers' Group, n.d.), p. 2.
4. Boston Women's Teachers' Group et al., "Effects of Institutional Structure," p. 12.

Selected Bibliography

Readers interested in pursuing some of the topics discussed in the text will find the following suggestions helpful points of departure:

On *preunderstanding,* see Bowers, Gadamer, Marx, Polanyi
On *critical social science,* see Bernstein, Bredo and Feinberg, Connerton, Habermas, Schroyer
On *dialogue,* see Freire, Habermas
On *testing,* see Gould, Kamin
On *teaching as management,* see Callahan
On *reproduction,* see Anyon, Apple and King, Bowles and Gintis, Willis

Anyon, Jean. "Social Class and the Hidden Curriculum of Work," *Journal of Education* (Winter 1980).

Apple, Michael. *Education and Power.* Boston: Routledge, Kegan Paul, 1982.

Apple, Michael. *Ideology and Curriculum.* Boston: Routledge, Kegan Paul, 1979.

Apple, Michael, and King, Nancy. "What Do Schools Teach?," *Curriculum Inquiry,* No. 4 (1977).

Bernstein, Richard. *Restructuring Social and Political Theory.* Philadelphia: University of Pennsylvania Press, 1976.

Bowers, C.A. "The Reproduction of Technological Consciousness: Locating the Ideological Foundations of a Radical Pedagogy," *Teachers College Record* (Summer 1982).

Bowles, Samuel, and Gintis, Herbert. *Schooling in Capitalist America.* New York: Basic Books, 1976.

Bredo, Eric, and Feinberg, Walter, eds. *Knowledge and Values in Social and Educational Research.* Philadelphia: Temple University Press, 1982.

Callahan, Raymond E. *Education and the Cult of Efficiency.* Chicago: University of Chicago Press, 1962.

Connerton, Paul, ed. *Critical Sociology*. New York: Penguin Books, 1976.

Freire, Paulo. *Education for Critical Consciousness*. Translated by Myra Bergman Ramos. New York: Continuum Publishing, 1982. First printing, 1973.

Freire, Paulo. *Pedagogy of the Oppressed*. Translated by Myra Bergman Ramos. New York: Herder and Herder, 1970.

Gadamer, Hans-George. *Philosophical Hermeneutics*. Berkeley: University of California Press, 1976.

Gould, Stephen Jay. *The Mismeasure of Man*. New York: W. W. Norton, 1981.

Habermas, Jurgen. *Communication and the Evolution of Society*. Translated by Thomas McCarthy. Boston: Beacon Press, 1976.

Habermas, Jurgen. *Knowledge and Human Interests*. Translated by Jeremy J. Shapiro. Boston: Beacon Press, 1971.

Habermas, Jurgen. *Legitimation Crisis*. Translated by Thomas McCarthy. Boston: Beacon Press, 1975.

Habermas, Jurgen. *Toward a Rational Society: Student Protest, Science and Politics*. Translated by Jeremy J. Shapiro. Boston: Beacon Press, 1970.

Kamin, Leon. *The Science and Politics of IQ*. New York: John Wiley and Sons, 1974.

Marx, Karl. "Bruno Bauer, On the Jewish Question," *Karl Marx Early Writings*. Translated and edited by T.B. Bottomore. New York: McGraw-Hill Book Company, 1964.

Marx, Karl. *Capital*, Vol. 1. New York: International Publishers, 1967.

Marx, Karl. *The Economic and Philosophic Manuscripts of 1844*. New York: International Publishers, 1964.

Marx, Karl, and Engels, Frederick. *The German Ideology*. New York: International Publishers, 1970.

McCarthy, Thomas. *The Critical Theory of Jurgen Habermas*. Cambridge, Mass.: MIT Press, 1978.

Polanyi, Michael. *Personal Knowledge*. Chicago: University of Chicago Press, 1962.

Polanyi, Michael. *The Study of Man*. Chicago: University of Chicago Press, 1958.

Schroyer, Trent. *The Critique of Domination*. Boston: Beacon Press, 1975.

Willis, Paul. *Learning to Labor: How Working Class Kids Get Working Class Jobs*. New York: Columbia University Press, 1981.

Index

"Our traditional liberal arts emphasis on esthetic, moral, and cognitive education has been replaced by a concern for training modeled on a factory-production view of control and efficiency. In short, with our current emphasis on training, we have reached the educational limits of the structures we have created to carry our educational ideals to fruition. Our mindedness now limits our ability to think and act in fresh ways and to grow cognitively, esthetically, and morally. Other visions of possibility are necessary." So write the authors of **Human Interests in the Curriculum: Teaching and Learning in a Technological Society**, a critical study of the influence of technical values on schooling and school life.

Throughout the book the authors unravel the complex manner in which the institutional structures of schools help to form and reinforce attitudes and beliefs that are hostile to human freedom and development. Five school programs that are national in scope and intent are examined. The authors raise questions about the taken-for-granted orientations of such programs to show that the effect of this "technocratic-mindedness" has been the emergence of a constricted view of the meaning of education and of the possible approaches to creating educative environments.

The authors point out that education can be emancipatory rather than limiting when it emphasizes communicative interaction. They show how the need for control in the classroom has secured a tyrannous hold over schooling, and explore the possibilities of challenging that tyranny.

This book will be of interest to undergraduate and graduate students of educational foundations and curriculum, as well as to teachers at all levels.

Robert V. Bullough, Jr. is associate professor of educational studies, **Stanley L. Goldstein** is visiting assistant professor of the philosophy of education, and **Ladd Holt** is associate professor of educational studies, all at the University of Utah.

Also of Interest—
TEACHING FOR COMPETENCE
Howard Sullivan and Norman Higgins
1983/Paper, ISBN 0-8077-2725-3

TEACHERS COLLEGE PRESS
Teachers College
Columbia University
New York, NY 10027

ISBN 0-8077-2745-8